Rabbi Mark Goldsmith

# Thirty-Six Words

Finding a balance between being a good Jew and a good global citizen.

Hadassa Word Press

**Imprint**
Any brand names and product names mentioned in this book are subject to trademark, brand or patent protection and are trademarks or registered trademarks of their respective holders. The use of brand names, product names, common names, trade names, product descriptions etc. even without a particular marking in this work is in no way to be construed to mean that such names may be regarded as unrestricted in respect of trademark and brand protection legislation and could thus be used by anyone.

Cover image: Provided by the author

Publisher:
Hadassa Word Press
is a trademark of
International Book Market Service Ltd., member of OmniScriptum Publishing Group
17 Meldrum Street, Beau Bassin 71504, Mauritius

Printed at: see last page
ISBN: 978-3-639-79515-8

**For Nicola, Alice and Miriam**

with appreciation for your patience, love and constant support

*All your children shall be taught to know God,*
*and great shall be the peace of your children. (Isaiah 54:13)*

*Read not* banayich, *your children,*
*but* bonayich, *your builders. (Berachot 64a)*

# CONTENTS

Forewords by *Rabbi Laura Janner-Klausner* and *Rabbi Josh Levy* ........ iii

Author's Note ................................................................. vi

Introduction ................................................................. vii

**Jewish Ethics**

What Has God Got To Do With The Time I Spend At Work? ............ 2

On Being An Unethical Monotheist ..................................... 7

The Meaning Of Success ................................................. 11

Judaism As Protest Against The Abuse Of Power ..................... 15

The Chimpanzee Warrior ................................................ 19

How Faiths Invest Their Assets ........................................ 24

Kiddush Hashem ......................................................... 29

**Jewish Global Concern**

The Ocean Is A Wilderness ............................................. 35

Don't Panic! This World May Be An Experiment ...................... 40

Please, No Plastic Fruit In Our Sukkah .............................. 44

Degrees Of Charity In The Twenty-First Century ..................... 49

The Beginning Of A New Era ............................................ 54

Jewish Trade Should Be Fair Trade .................................... 59

**Jewish Memory and Texts**

It's Not For The Survivors To Remember ............................... 65

Mind Your Language ..................................................... 70

Telling Stories Of The Past For A Better Future ..................... 75

The Value Of Hebrew .................................................... 79

Making History In Eighty Metres ...................................... 84

The Not-Messiah Of Golders Green ..................................... 89

## Jewish Ritual

The Meaning Of Kashrut For Today ....................................................95
No Cathedrals In Judaism Please......................................................101
It Would Not Really Have Been Enough............................................106
Thank God As Well As The Caterer...................................................110
The Not Mitzvah.................................................................................115
Shabbat Technology? .........................................................................119

## Jewish Society

Our Ketubah With Society .................................................................124
When The Wilderness Is Good For You .............................................128
The Everlasting Congregation Does Not Exist..................................132
Women Rabbis ...................................................................................136
Finding The Perfect Rabbi.................................................................141
Every Life Has Its Ups And Downs ...................................................146
Who Would Have Thought That Religion Would Still Be A Player? ..150

## Jewish Thought

The Fundamental Truth Is A Lie .......................................................156
Who Has Kept Judaism Going All These Years?................................161
The Fruitless Search For An Easy Life..............................................167
Will The Real Monotheist Please Stand Up?.....................................171

Index...................................................................................................176
Index of biblical and rabbinic text references...................................178
Glossary..............................................................................................181
Bibliography.......................................................................................188

# Forewords

IF YOU WANT a book on Judaism that manages to be inspirational, understandable and have depth, this collection of thirty-six nuggets of Torah is the one for you. Written by the erudite, articulate and astoundingly compassionate Rabbi Mark Goldsmith, this collection of thirty-six "words" of Torah (*Divrei Torah*) can be read chapter by chapter but it is also beautifully written to dip in and out of whilst you commute or just want to sprinkle your day with Jewish/Torah inspiration.

Rabbi Goldsmith manages to write theology with a gentle touch which is both wise and unintimidating. I love how these teachings of Torah bring together day to day, mundane and common experiences and then enhance them with an immensely wide spectrum of Jewish knowledge. You can be stimulated by intellect that is without a trace of pomposity. This is a rare gift for someone who has had such a distinguished rabbinic career over the last twenty years.

*Thirty-Six Words* provides us with the ability to understand Reform Judaism, to appreciate what makes us tick and what distinguishes us from other streams of Judaism. Rabbi Goldsmith interweaves the universal utopian vision of Jewish encounters with the world with the strong, particular, Jewish, progressive vision of equality, social justice and the balance of mercy and justice that lies at the core of Judaism.

However, don't be fooled, Rabbi Goldsmith will not leave you unchanged or unchallenged. He might have a gentle style but much of the content is dynamite – his call to recognise that we are stewards of God's world ends with the wise words, "the days of taking the Earth for granted are over". He knows that the task of Jews is to improve, heal, transform the world and he unequivocally calls on us to play our part in this work, human work, Jewish work, God's work.

I wish you, dear reader, a pleasant journey through these thirty-six stimulating interpretations of Torah, but please be aware that the final destination of this book will alter your future journeys.

*Rabbi Laura Janner-Klausner*
*Senior Rabbi to the Movement for Reform Judaism*

A BOOK OF this kind, compiled from twenty years of thinking and writing in the congregational rabbinate, is not merely a collection of pieces *by* an author, but is a document *about* the author. It is about who he is, the issues that inspire him, his concerns and frustrations. Through the words on the page we can feel and understand the principles that underpin his approach to his Judaism and his vocation.

The foundation of Mark's rabbinate is a strong belief about what Judaism can and should be: that it should inspire us to think about our own lives, and that the rabbinic role is to bridge the gap between ancient tradition and modern life to ensure that Judaism is relevant to the tasks of today; that this requires a Judaism that is substantial, filled with content, thoughtful, never simplistic. This belief infuses these writings.

So, too, does Mark's commitment to the life of the spirit. His is not a prescriptive spirituality, one which tells us "how to be spiritual", but one that is open and diverse, attempting to meet every individual where they are. It is not a self-indulgent spirituality, only for the benefit of the individual, but one rooted in community, and in a belief in our ability to impact on the world around us.

Most of all, perhaps, what comes through is Mark's dedication. The quality of sermons, of teaching, that he has aspired to over twenty years has never wavered. He believes he owes the very best of himself to his congregants whenever he can.

These ideals are found throughout the pages of this book. They are there, too, in the community that we are proud to build together.

*Rabbi Josh Levy*
*Alyth (North Western Reform) Synagogue, London*

# Author's Note

At the back of this book there is an index to most of the topics covered. There is also an index to the Torah verses quoted and other biblical and rabbinic texts which appear in the pieces. Next is a Glossary which explains over one-hundred of the less commonly used terms in this book. The short Bibliography refers only to books which are directly quoted in the text.

For transliterations of Hebrew to English characters this book generally follows the system used in *Seder HaTefillot: Forms of Prayer*, the edition of the Siddur of the Movement for Reform Judaism published in 2008. Occasionally, more colloquial transliterations are used for very common words. Hebrew words which are commonly used in English writings are not italicised, those less commonly used are.

The pieces aim not to use gendered language except where unavoidable for the sense of a sentence. Then the gender of a pronoun should not be taken to be exclusive of the other gender.

For dates the book uses CE for Common Era where the conventional usage is AD, and BCE for Before the Common Era where the conventional usage is BC. This usage is explained further in the Glossary.

# Introduction

THE BOOK OF Deuteronomy, the final book of the Torah, begins *Eileh HaDevarim*, these are the words which Moses spoke to all Israel. What then follows is a reinterpretation of the whole Torah narrative which preceded. In its own setting, Deuteronomy is Moses remembering and telling a new generation of Israelites what happened on their journey from Egypt to the borders of the Promised Land, and the principles, laws and religious structures which would then build their society when they established it there. Some of the story is a little different from that which is recorded in the preceding books of the Torah, the principles are more clearly stated, the laws are, it seems, updated, and the religious structure is now to centre on a single worship space. It is almost as if these thirty-four chapters of Deuteronomy are themselves a *D'var Torah*, an individual interpretation of Torah from Moses himself.

Biblical critics suggest that the basis for the Book of Deuteronomy is a reform of Judaism in the seventh century BCE under King Josiah, reframing the developing nation and religion to centralise it and reign in diversity of Jewish practice, and telling the history differently too, from a later point of view. They identify the Book of Deuteronomy with the book "discovered" in the underused Temple in the Second Book of Kings, chapter 22, in the time of King Josiah.

Whichever way you understand it then, the opening words of Deuteronomy tell you that you are about to hear an interpretation of words of Torah, a *D'var Torah*. The thirty-six pieces in this book all have their origin as *Divrei Torah*. They were given orally originally in a number of synagogues, most at Alyth (North Western Reform)

Synagogue, some at Finchley Progressive Synagogue and a few at Woodford Progressive Synagogue (now Woodford Liberal Synagogue), the three congregations which I have served in my twenty years so far as a congregational rabbi. They have been edited and rewritten especially for this collection.

A *D'var Torah* is the opportunity to add your own voice to millennia of Torah interpretation. When I read Torah I do so as a Jew brought up in the Progressive Jewish tradition, the fifth generation of my family to be so. My learning has been built on a foundation of Liberal and Reform rabbis and teachers. This means that whilst the particular in Judaism is very important to me, so that Jewish peoplehood moulds who I am, Jewish texts inform me and I am always seeking my place in Jewish history and practice, the universal is always pulling me to ask why Jewishness matters in the world, giving me a mission to bring the strengths of Judaism to a broader community and to contribute to Judaism's potential to be a "light to the nations".

Particularism and universalism are at either end of a spectrum of the meaning of Judaism. Too much particularism and Judaism is reduced to the practices of a tribe whose existence and contribution is easily irrelevant to God's world. Too much universalism and Judaism disappears into vague hopes of universal peace and unity with nothing sound underneath and no programme to help make it happen. As a proud Progressive Jew, I am always trying to find a place of balance between the two.

This collection of thirty-six pieces is thus divided into six sections, all of which include a measure of the particular and the universal: Jewish Ethics, considering how the ethical teachings of Judaism can enable us to interact with the world around us; Jewish Global Concern, considering how Judaism might make us better global citizens in a world more connected than our ancestors could ever have imagined; Jewish Memory and Texts, considering how our lived and recorded past as Jews inform our present; Jewish Ritual, considering how the actions of Judaism can come into the present day and future; Jewish Society, considering the developments in Jewish community life which encourage us and challenge us, and finally Jewish Thought, considering how the thought underlying Judaism informs us today.

There is a mystical concept that there are, at any one time in the world, thirty-six people, *lammed vavniks*, who live undiscovered lives and who, if only truly empowered to make change, could bring about the Messianic Age. The Hebrew letter *lammed* has the value of thirty and *vav* the value of six. The idea behind the *lammed vavniks*, as I read it, is that the world is always capable of change, life can get better at all levels, but the route towards this is tough to discover, it lies in unexpected places through unexpected people.

The number thirty-six can also be made up from the Hebrew letters *alef, lammed* and *heh,* the letters which make up the word *eileh,* of *eileh hadevarim,* these are the words, hence thirty-six words. Since the next words of the opening of Deuteronomy are *asher diber Mosheh,* which Moses spoke, and my Hebrew name is *Mosheh,* I hope that I will be forgiven for putting thirty-six pieces together which express one Jew's voice and naming them for these words.

Each of the pieces is short, under two thousand words. In compiling them I imagined the reader having the time of a London Underground train journey from Finchley, where I live, to Euston in the West End of London. Time to read something that might be thought-provoking and which would give a perspective on Torah. They are straightforward pieces, not based on deep scholarship but based as soundly as I can on a lifetime of loving Torah and our classical Jewish texts. They are like the straight lines and consistent angles of Harry Beck's original 1933 map of the London Underground, the template for all other maps of the Underground since. This Finchley-based draughtsman made a simple guide to something much more complex in the street layout above, in the year that Alyth Synagogue was founded. It is itself the beginning of a journey, as are these thirty-six pieces.

That is my aim for this book. That it helps the reader to take a step on the journey of Jewish life, in a place of balance between the particular and the universal. That reader may be a *lammed vavnik* themselves. They may be able to pick up ideas here that help them to make change. That reader may be able to use some of the ideas and sources here to create their own *Divrei Torah*, their own voice which adds to the richness of Torah for the future.

*Rabbi Mark Goldsmith, London, 2019/5779*

# Jewish Ethics

1

# What Has God Got To Do With The Time I Spend At Work?

ON THE WALL of a friend's dining room they have one of those popular prints taken from papers like the *Illustrated London News* from the mid-nineteenth century. The print shows a nineteenth-century gentleman dressed in country gear walking along a rural lane through a wooded area, with a wooded hill gently sloping to his right. There are no houses, not even a horse and carriage to impede his country walk. The caption of the picture is "Kilburn High Road looking towards Hampstead". It does not look much like that anymore. Today Kilburn High Road is one of the most built-up parts of London.

I'm sure that many of us have prints of towns and cities of the past, perhaps the areas in which we live as they appeared a couple of hundred years ago. When you look at them they all share something in common, the skyline is dominated by the churches and cathedrals, if London, then the dome of St Paul's Cathedral and the many other Wren churches that punctuate the cityscape of London.

Today, if you picture a city, it is never the churches, the houses of God so to speak, that define the skyline. Rather it is the houses of mammon, the office building skyscrapers which give shape to our cities: for London, the BT Tower, Canary Wharf, the Shard and the Gherkin. Only strict planning requirements have saved St Paul's the ignominy of being completely obscured from view.

When the prophet Balaam looked out from the summit of Peor over the plains of Moab to see the children of Israel encamped he said, *mah tovu ohalecha ya'kcov, mishk'notecha yisra'el*, how beautiful are the tents of Jacob, your dwelling places O Israel, both in the plural.[1] What would he say if he were to stand on the terrace at Alexandra Palace and look out over London?

---

[1] Numbers 24:5

Would he be able to declare that what he sees is a thing of beauty? He would see the places where we work dominating his view. And what he would see would quite accurately reflect the balance of the lives of those of us of working age. People in London work on average very long hours compared to elsewhere in Europe, and even compared to anywhere else in the country. Londoners work for an average of 9.5 hours a day with an average working week in the city of 54 hours. If you are the head of one of these companies then things are even more of a strain. Fully half of the heads of British companies say that they never make it home during the week in time to see their school-age children. A similar survey carried out in France found only 25% of company bosses saying they never made it home to see their children, and of Spanish bosses only 12% did not make it home in time to see their children during the week.

Clearly Londoners have developed for themselves a tough work ethic. A number of members of our synagogue held a debate at our *Bayit Cham* lunch after the Shabbat service between the lunchers, who were mostly aged well over seventy, and the helpers who were under twenty. The issue was, "Would it be better to be growing up today or at the time that you were children?" The almost unanimous answer was that it had been better to grow up pre-war, as elders agreed that our long working hours and ever-increasing material expectations were creating a poorer experience of life than they had when they were in their younger years.

We human beings have definite meaning to our lives according to teachings of Judaism. Our purpose is to try to imitate God. As it says in the Midrash Sifre: "Just as God is gracious and compassionate, we must be gracious and compassionate, just as God is beneficent and loving, so must we be beneficent and loving."[2] But God is also, in our understanding, creative and hard working. As Bachya Ibn Pakuda wrote in eleventh-century Spain: "The active participation of Man in the creation of his wealth is a sign of his spiritual greatness. In this respect he imitates God."[3]

---

[2] Sifre Deuteronomy 49
[3] Jeffrey Salkin, *Being God's Partner* (Woodstock: Jewish Lights, 1994), p63

But we are not God and nor can we be God, rather God is our role model. Herein, perhaps, lies the problem. God has all eternity to achieve what He purposes. God can be in an infinite number of places at one time. God can be expected to know everything and to take responsibility for everything. God has no body and thus does not need to worry about His health and, at least in Judaism, has no children to try and get home in time to see. Indeed God does not even have a home to return to and can remain at His post all the time. If we consider the working habits of many of what we consider are the high achievers in our society we can see that their drivenness encourages them to work as if imitating all these non-human aspects of God. Perhaps the one piece of God's make-up that they do not try to imitate is that God always, without fail, takes a day off every week – the Shabbat! The end result of working like this is not terribly praiseworthy. No-one ever said on their death bed, "I wish I had spent more time at the office."

To make life worthwhile we have to try to achieve balance in our lives, validating our existence not only through our work but just as much through our relationships, our home life, our leisure and study. It is not difficult to find where Judaism fits into the latter four of these. Our relationships are influenced by Judaism's values of love, respect for the other, commitment and care. Our home life includes Jewish rituals to sanctify the home and the concept that the home is a *mikdash me'at*, a small sanctuary, where we can join our family to live the best of our lives. Our leisure is established by our duty to rest on the Shabbat and study is a fundamental Jewish duty in order to make our Judaism meaningful at all, and certainly to make it grow beyond childhood conceptions. But since we do spend so much time at work, does Judaism leave us there? Is God with us at work as He is in our relationships, our home life, our leisure and our study?

Our answer must be based on the assertion that Judaism is not a hobby to be squeezed into spare moments at weekends but rather that it is a life-orienting set of values and teachings to help give eternal value to everything that we do. Jews are not commanded to be spiritual, rather they are required to do something positive in this world with their spirit and body together, that is, to bring the world to a point of holiness. We are God's hands to achieve the mission of Judaism in this world.

As Meir Tamari notes, out of the 613 commandments that our sages identified in the Torah, well over a hundred are connected with our economic life, our life at work. Only twenty or so of the 613 are connected, for example, with keeping kosher, often seen by some as the gold standard of Judaism. These economic *mitzvot* are expressed in terms that might seem to be archaic, like leaving the corners of your field for the poor and the stranger to glean. But all are transferable to the current work situation with a little imagination and effort. How, for example, might one bring holiness into the workplace in the way we employ and work with staff?

The Torah tells us just to pay our hired hands on time[4] and, when we free a slave, to send them off with enough to sustain them for a while: "And when you send him out free from you, you shall not let him go away empty, give him some of your flock and the produce of your threshing floor and winepress", in recognition of how he has been a partner in God's blessing to you of wealth.[5] It takes a small leap of imagination to recognise that holiness at work, bringing Judaism and God into your workplace, asks you, through the principles based on these texts, to recognise and value the whole lives of those who work for you even for a day. Judaism teaches that a person must not be used as an expendable commodity. There is no such thing in Judaism as "Human Resources". Then, for those who have worked for you for some years and have been part of your ability to provide for your family, when that relationship comes to an end, through redundancy or for whatever reason, to give them a portion of what they have helped you to create, in order to set them on their way with recognition of their value. Text-message sackings are not Godly.

---

[4] Leviticus 19:13
[5] Deuteronomy 15:14

In the Midrash on the book of Numbers an interpretation is offered of the priestly blessing, "May God bless you and keep you."[6] What is the difference between being blessed and being kept or guarded by God? The answer offered is this – May God bless you with wealth and possessions. May God keep you from being taken over by this wealth and these possessions and the desire for them.[7] Our work is part of ourselves and our value as Jews. It can take us over if we let it and drive us far from God, or we can bring God to it and make the days that we labour and do all of our work the time when our Judaism is most with us.

---

[6] Numbers 6:24
[7] Bemidbar Rabbah 11:5

# On Being An Unethical Monotheist

ONE OF MY favourite places on Earth is called Paradise. It is a study institute in Jerusalem which goes by the Hebrew name of Pardes. It is open to everyone and teaches a brand of respect for traditional texts, together with a deep concern for the real world around us. The word Pardes, as well as meaning Paradise, can be read as an acronym for the four traditional ways of studying a Jewish text: *P'shat* – the surface meaning; *Remez* – hints that you can find in the text to a deeper meaning; *D'rash* – the Midrashim which you can draw out of interpreting the text; and *Sod* – the mystical meaning or trying to discern God's inspiration behind the text. At Pardes, near Emek Refaim in Jerusalem, you get to do all of these. I have been there many times both physically and virtually through their podcast series, which is the most popular Jewish Bible study podcast in the world.

The spiritual guide of Pardes is Rabbi Meir Shweiger. Many young adults will spend a few months studying at Pardes. Rabbi Shweiger helps them gain spiritual growth from the experience. He writes of one young man who came to Pardes looking like any lightly observant Jew but who after a while began to wear a kippah, the traditional Jewish skull cap, regularly to classes and around the institute and the cafes and shops around. Rabbi Shweiger met him on a bus some way into his study stay at Pardes, minus kippah. No big deal. Pardes is not a coercive yeshivah. Back at the Institute, Rabbi Shweiger asked the young man why he did not wear a kippah on the bus.

The young man's answer was this: "If I wear a kippah in public like on the bus and say an elderly disabled person gets on and I don't give up my seat then I feel that I will be doing dishonour to religious Judaism. She will think badly of religious Jews because of my actions." Rabbi Shweiger did a double take at the backwards logic and then said back, "You know, it sounds to me like you'd better wear the kippah on the bus – then you would actually get up and give up your seat!"

When appearing religious does not go with decent ethics it is a very clear breach of the third commandment: "Do not take the name of your Eternal God in vain."[8] When an outside of ritual covers an inside of arrogance and thoughtlessness the basics of what it means to be a Jew are missing. Balaam, one of the anti-heroes of the Torah, is a case in point. Balaam ended up blessing the Children of Israel and being unable to crush their morale, but before that he was prepared, for enough money, to go and curse them as a hired prophet. After that he turned against the Israelites and died in battle fighting against them in the army of the Midianites. But, notes Rabbi Pinchas Kahn,[9] there is something remarkable about Balaam beyond the donkey incident, where even his donkey seemed to be more attuned to decent spiritual ethics than this famous prophet.[10]

From the very first time that we meet Balaam in the Bible he says that he is a follower of Adonai, God.[11] He uses the language of Jewish piety whilst doing a number of distinctly unethical things. You could call Balaam an unethical monotheist.

Perhaps this is why the donkey is so important in his story. After all, just like Abraham in the story of the binding of his son Isaac, and using exactly the same Hebrew words, Balaam wakes up early in the morning to curse the Israelites and saddles his donkey, just as Abraham wakes up early in the morning to follow the command of God, and also enthusiastically saddles his donkey for the journey.[12] In Balaam's story the donkey then needs to tell him what he should be doing. Abraham knows himself, no talking donkeys needed. Whilst Balaam intends but fails to curse the Israelites and cause their destruction by the Moabite army, Abraham argues with God for the preservation of the people of Sodom and Gomorrah, despite their rough treatment of his own family.[13]

---

[8] Exodus 20:7
[9] Pinchas Kahn, *Jewish Bible Quarterly*, Autumn 2007
[10] Numbers 22:22ff
[11] Eg. Numbers 22:8
[12] Genesis 22:3
[13] Genesis 18:20ff

Arguing with God for the ethical thing to be done is the ultimate in ethical monotheism.

Ethical monotheism means that, because there is God and because there is one God, that God commands a way of living in which there is one standard of ethics. There is one decent way of treating people and the world around us. The task of finding that way is tough. It is very noticeable that the places in which Progressive and Orthodox Jews interact and work together most comfortably are in those areas of Jewish life where we need to discover together the ethical way of living in the modern world, in Jewish Medical, Social, Environmental and Business Ethics.

There is another unethical character in the Bible who uses the name of God to establish his credentials as a religious Jew. That is Laban, like Balaam a wandering Aramean. Laban is the man who tricks his nephew Jacob into marrying the daughter he had not intended to, and who nearly gets away with employing Jacob for twenty-one years with no pay. Laban, too, uses God's name a number of times in his narrative, but he is also worshipping numerous idols and treats Jacob very shoddily.[14]

Our rituals and piety have a feeling of eternity to them. It is straightforward to transmit tradition and love of God by lighting Shabbat candles, by reading and learning to read Torah, by saying our traditional prayers. That is our monotheism. What is more challenging is responding in the best way to the ethical challenges that we face pretty much every day, to trade fairly, to give up some of our best for the benefit of the disadvantaged, to make the right decision in the care of a sick person, to keep gossip to yourself, and also to give up a seat on a crowded tube train or a bus in Jerusalem when we see someone struggling.

When we struggle with the right ethical response and, having found it, carry it through into action, then we are serving God. The prophet Micah

---

[14] For example Genesis 30:27 and 31:49

is clear in his response to the polarities of ritual and ethics which pole we should favour: "Will the Eternal be pleased with thousands of rams, or with ten thousands of rivers of oil? Shall I give my firstborn for my transgression, the fruit of my body for the sin of my soul? He has told you, every one of you, what is good; and what does the Eternal require of you, but to do justice, and to love mercy, and to walk humbly with your God?"[15] That's the way to paradise.

---

[15] Micah 6:6-8

# The Meaning Of Success

PERHAPS IT IS down to careful planning or perhaps it is by chance, but some of us are given the opportunity to say just before we die something of great profundity that is never forgotten. As the poet Lord Byron drew his last breaths he said sweetly, "Now I shall go to sleep, Goodnight." Queen Elizabeth I expressed a thought that would strike a chord for all of us, "All my possessions for a moment of time", just before her final moment. Lady Nancy Astor, seeing all her family gathered around her bed in her last minutes, woke briefly to say, "Am I dying or is this my birthday?" Surely Oscar Wilde must have planned his last utterance – so characteristic was it of the great humourist: "Either that wallpaper goes or I do."

Spike Milligan, one of the greatest comedians of the past century, definitely planned his. They are inscribed on his tombstone in a graveyard in Winchelsea in Irish Gaelic (he was born in Ireland), "*Duirt me leat go raibh me breoite*", not what he said but what he had always planned for his epitaph. In English it means, "I told you I was ill."

It is inevitable that we should put great significance into last words, especially if they convey something about the character of the person whom we have lost. Many of us will have recorded somewhere our first words, in baby books perhaps. For me it was "Utty", the closest I could manage to "Sooty", the actual name of our cat.

I suspect that most of us know the first words of the Bible: "*Bereshit Bara Elohim et ha shamayim v'et ha'aretz*", In the beginning God created the Heavens and the Earth.[16] But how many of us know the last words of the Bible? Just what they are is slightly controversial depending on whether you go for the order of the Hebrew Bible preserved in the Christian Bible, where the Bible ends with Malachi, the last prophet, and his words about

---

[16] Genesis 1:1

11

the end of the world and Elijah's return,[17] or whether you go with the order given in every Jewish Bible published since the early centuries of the Common Era, where the last book of the Bible is the Book of Chronicles. What are the Hebrew Bible's not quite so famous last words?

They concern the exile of the Jews to Babylonia from Judah and how their seventy years in exile, "fulfil the word of the Eternal by the mouth of Jeremiah, until the land had enjoyed her Sabbaths; for as long as she lay desolate she kept Sabbath, to fulfil seventy years." And finally how Cyrus the king of Persia allowed the Jews to return to their land to rebuild the Temple.[18]

The economy of Israel was to be built in a particular way. There was to be hard work to gain the best fruits of the land but every seven years it was to be left fallow to recover its strength as agricultural land, a Sabbath for the land. Every seven times seven years the land itself was, through the Jubilee, to return to its original tribal holders so that land accumulation in the hands of a few families did not happen.[19] Earlier in the Book of Leviticus it was stressed that every seven days there was to be a day of human and animal rest when nothing new was created and that, of every field we own and crop that we grow, a portion was to be set aside for the poor and the stranger to glean and feed themselves for free.[20]

The last words of the Bible say that, because we did not observe these laws, but kept hold of everything for ourselves, we were driven out of the land and kept out for seventy years to make up for the time of our greed. From observing the laws of Leviticus and their spirit in our time come blessings, very special blessings, not only of prosperity but of being satisfied with that prosperity and living in safety and security to enjoy it, and living in a way which is the opposite of being a slave, truly free.

---

[17] Malachi 4:24
[18] 2 Chronicles 36:21f
[19] Leviticus 25:1-24
[20] Leviticus 19:9-10

Why? Because as Rabbi Yehoshua Engleman says, "If you hold onto something too tight the Bible says that you will lose it", just as the Jews lost their nation of Judah.

The Bible, in its last words, tells us clearly what failure for a society would be.

Failure is a society where selfish interests dominate, where everyone grabs for themselves and is unable to let anything go for the good of others. Success in the Bible is a society where people build their own prosperity, but in the context of giving themselves rest and those around them as well, where busyness is not constant but rather there are times and spaces to refresh ourselves.

Success is a society where the poor, the dispossessed and the stranger, meaning for us the refugee and the recent arrival, and those deeply disadvantaged in the world, can count on us with any level of prosperity to see that what we have is God's gift to us, earned with our God-given talents or through what we have been able to build on previous generations. Thus we do not fully own our prosperity, but rather some of it must be shared with those whose lives have not been as favoured as ours.

Success is a society where the country in which we live is cared for, the modern day equivalent of *Shmittah*, the seven-year lying fallow of the land. The Bible is clear that we can use the Earth's produce, but not without any limitation, not without ensuring that what is beautiful about it remains. Success is a society where in every succeeding generation there is enough opportunity to build prosperity. That is the message of the Jubilee. God is a sharing owner of the world and is unlike Pharaoh of Egypt who is an accumulating owner, trying to grab everything for himself.[21] We in the image of God should also ensure that our society enables all to share in prosperity in the long term.

---

[21] Genesis 47:20ff

In *Pirke Avot* there is a passage which speaks of four kinds of people with respect to how they treat what they have gained. The person who says "What is mine is mine and what is yours is yours" creates an unforgiving and uncaring society like that of Sodom in the book of Genesis.[22] One who says "What is mine is yours and what is yours is mine" creates a society that is unrealistic, the word used in the Hebrew means uneducated. The person who says "What is mine is mine and what is yours is mine" is wicked, accumulating all to themselves. But the person who says "What is mine is yours too and what is yours is yours" understands the true message of his religion, in Hebrew the word is *chassid*, because in this society no-one becomes destitute.[23]

When we aim to shape the future of our country we should be looking out for generosity of spirit, a care for all people, preservation of the land and a continued sharing of prosperity. Only in this way can we enjoy the blessings of which the Torah speaks. The awful alternative is to live behind walls, living in fear of the dispossessed, as has happened in a number of countries, notably in Brazil, Colombia and parts of South Africa. Rather, we should build a successful society of opportunity for all to reach their potential, so that we can be satisfied with what we have and live in security with each other.

The last words of the Bible say: fail to do this and expect trouble in the future. The first words of the Bible say: everything is possible in accord with what we understand as God's ideals for the world.

---

[22] Genesis 13:13ff
[23] Mishnah Avot 5:10

# Judaism As Protest Against The Abuse Of Power

A DESIGN CHALLENGE for you. Design something that produces oxygen, sequesters carbon, fixes nitrogen, distils water, accrues solar energy, creates complex sugar for foods, keeps soil in place, creates microclimates, changes colours with the seasons, and self-replicates. What is it? A tree.

Ok, so why don't we knock that down and write on it? Make it into a piece of paper. We can. But in our generation we know that if we do so to too great a scale then we denude the world of these remarkable and amazing resources with potentially catastrophic results. Cut down too many trees and soil erosion and carbon dioxide increase will ruin our living environment. Every year millions of acres of rainforest are lost. An average-sized pine tree can produce 80,000 pieces of A4 paper, but you would be amazed how much of the stuff we use, over 300 million tonnes per year worldwide. We must not abuse our power to harvest nature.

Next design challenge. Now design something that can love, create poetry, design things itself, communicate to any person, do complex mathematics, behave with care and compassion, build a house, think the deepest thoughts, bring up children, live within a religious system, make community, write, sing, dance. What is it? A person.

Now own one of them. Make them a slave. Restrict their movement, own their labour, trade in their children. No wonder the Israelites sing when they are released from captivity in Egypt as they cross the Sea of Reeds.[24] No wonder that freedom and the urge for liberation of all peoples is so central to Judaism.

The great challenge for humanity is that every one of us has the capacity to abuse the power in our hands. We have the power to despoil the

---

[24] Exodus Chapter 15

natural environment so easily. We have the power to control other people and remove their freedom from one day to the next.

At the root of Judaism is a continuous protest from generation to generation against the abuse of such power.

Judaism always recognises that within every one of us is a *yetzer tov*, an inclination to do good, and a *yetzer ra*, an inclination to do bad. No person is inherently good or evil. Our task as human beings is so to balance the two that we never abuse the power in our hands, so that our good inclination comes out on top. A measure of ambition and greed are necessary for the creativity to solve the world's challenges. Unless we have the urge to do better we will never be driven to cure others' diseases, to help with the problems and challenges suffered by others. But ambition and greed out of control lead to trampling upon other people, putting them into situations not so far off the slavery which Judaism condemns.

Very often in the Torah the social legislation is a protest against the abuse of power.

The Hebrew slave, who was normally a person who worked off his indebtedness by working for a period of years for his creditor, could not be kept in this condition for more than six years under any circumstances, save that he himself chose to remain in the household of his creditor.[25] An employer could not keep the wages of a worker overnight.[26] The employer has the power in this relationship, he must not abuse it. A lender could not keep hold of basic necessities as pledge for a loan, he had to return the clothing taken in pledge for his debtor to use on a cold night.[27] The wealthy and well-known could not abuse their power in the courts. Neither could the poor abuse the power of sympathy to escape justice when justice must be done.[28]

---

[25] Exodus 21:1-6
[26] Leviticus 19:13
[27] Exodus 22:25-26
[28] Exodus 23:3,6 and Leviticus 19:15

One of the most striking examples of Judaism's protest against the abuse of power is the Torah verse which says, "Do not follow a majority of people to do something bad."[29] When the whole of society seems to be doing something you cannot agree with, a Jew must go against the trend. This is our basic protection against popular racism, against destruction of the environment, against destructive tribalism.

God's place in Judaism is as the guarantor that abuse of human power will never triumph in the long term. The powerful who abuse their power will always fall. The message is driven home at the end of every Passover Seder service, when we gather as the Jewish family to celebrate that now we live in freedom, that we have come through the Sea of Reeds and we will never accept enslavement again, nor enslave others.

The final song of the Seder gives this message in code – it seems like a bit of fun but it is much more than that. It is *Chad Gadya*, a song in Aramaic about one goat (that is us, the Jewish people) whom our father (that is God) bought for two *zuzim* (that is the tablets of the Ten Commandments, representing Torah). In this song, which first appears in the fourteenth century, though first seen in print in a Haggadah in Prague in 1590, a dog beats a cat and a stick beats the dog and the fire burns the stick and the water quenches the fire and an ox drinks the water and the *shochet*, the slaughterer, kills the ox, and the *shochet* succumbs to the Angel of Death, but even this great power cannot reign for ever, for above all is the Holy One of Blessing, *Ha Kadosh Baruch Hu.*

Who are all these creatures among whom the Jews, the little goat, are blown like so much flotsam and jetsam? They are the empires which abused their power from generation to generation, eating each other up until the writer of *Chad Gadya* in the fourteenth century said let's not only celebrate our freedom from Pharoah's abuse of power but also that from all of the empires of humanity which oppressed us. The cat is Assyria, the dog is Babylon, the stick is Persia, the fire the Greek empire, the water the Romans, the ox the Muslim Caliphates, the *shochet* the

---

[29] Exodus 23:2

17

Crusaders and the Angel of Death the Ottomans. So far up to the fourteenth century! But the author of the song had confidence that somehow the Holy One of Blessing would stand behind Jewish values, that abuse of human power would always be challenged and never last.

This key Jewish value challenges each one of us. Are we careful about how we use our power in personal relationships, neither abusing our ability to influence nor submitting to the unacceptable? Do we properly balance our power in business so that we do not exploit suppliers or let down customers? Do we ask of our politicians that our country be fair to the needs of all? Do we support Israel, the place in the world where Jews have substantial political power, to exercise its power with compassion and ambition for the peoples who live under its control, Jews and Arabs alike? Do we enjoy the fruits of nature with consideration for a sustainable future not only for ourselves but also for the poorest of the world, whose natural environment can be so degraded by our consumption of their resources?

The essential Jewish narrative is of a people who have not only left slavery behind but who have also taken on responsibility as partners of the Holy One of Blessing, *Ha Kadosh Baruch Hu*.

# The Chimpanzee Warrior

IF YOUR LIFE expectancy is forty-five years, is it worth dying over fig trees? In the Kibale national park in Uganda large groups of males strike out in silent single-file patrols to expand the number of fig trees under their control. Between 1999 and 2008 eighteen were killed in violent attacks during these patrols. Most of the victims were teenagers. Mothers and children too were beaten as the raiders snatched and killed their offspring. No-one on either side was starving, but the raiders managed to increase their lands in the fig-tree area by more than a fifth.

You might ask, how could human beings be so cruel as to fight like this over a luxury? The answer: in this case they are not. The single-file patrols, the raiders, the killers and the victims are all chimpanzees. The study which witnessed this violent behaviour was conducted by John Mitani of the University of Michigan over a decade and what he found might tell us more about ourselves than we find comfortable.[30]

Hunter-gatherer societies among humans are the most violent in the world, not city societies. According to Steven Pinker, Professor of Psychology at Harvard, if you live as a hunter-gatherer in Papua New Guinea today, you have a more than one-in-six chance of dying at the hands of another man, as disputes erupt over territories.[31] Studying current hunter-gatherer tribes, the proportion of male adults who die in violence is extraordinary, from 20% to 60% of all males. Even during the violent twentieth century, with two World Wars, less than 2% of males worldwide died in warfare.

The Ngogo group of chimpanzees in the Kibale National Park are even more violent than hunter-gatherers. A chimpanzee is even more likely to die in violence between chimp and chimp.

---

[30] Study from *Current Biology*, quoted in *The Economist*, 26 June 2010
[31] Steven Pinker, *Ted Talks – A History of Violence*, 2007

Does the chimpanzee society tell us that for humans to be violent is just a natural drive? There is another key finding of the University of Michigan study, that chimpanzees do not fight alone. Rather they maintain "complex, collaborative social networks, suggesting that only by bonding within groups can chimps engage in violence between such groups."

John Mitani suggests that it may be that our ability to bond with strangers was forged originally by the demands of war, of fighting to defend or extend our territory. He also suggests that the "human tendency to coalesce around abstract concepts such as religion or nation, which underpins civilisation, may well be an evolutionary legacy of a violent past." After all, this is what brings chimpanzees together and somehow enables them to communicate with each other enough to go on patrol and expand their territories with respect to other chimpanzee groups.

In evolutionary terms the line leading to chimpanzees or to humans split five million years ago. Humans have continued to bond with strangers. Humans have also continued to come together for a purpose: consider Judaism.

How did we leave the violent impulse behind? Indeed have we? These chilling words in the Book of Deuteronomy begin with the same *Shema Yisrael* that starts the prayer on the lips of every observant Jew twice a day:

"Hear, O Israel; You are to pass over the Jordan this day, to go in to possess nations greater and mightier than yourself, cities great and fortified up to Heaven, A people great and tall, the sons of the Anakim, whom you know, and of whom you have heard say, Who can stand before the sons of Anak! Understand therefore this day, that the Eternal your God is he who goes over before you; as a consuming fire he shall destroy them, and he shall bring them down before your face; so shall you drive them out, and destroy them quickly, as the Eternal has said to you."[32]

These passages, and others like them which we read from the Book of Deuteronomy, are not the direction which Judaism took in the millennia which followed. Whilst our founding ethos in the Torah is undoubtedly one of a people struggling like the Ngogo chimpanzees to establish its territory with all the means at its disposal, Judaism developed away from this ethos. The Prophet Isaiah told us that the Jewish dream was not of becoming great warriors but rather of peace, of a day when "swords shall be beaten into ploughshares and spears into pruning hooks."[33] When "They shall not hurt not destroy in all my holy mountain."[34]

Peace not strength became the greatest blessing. As Rabbi Simeon Bar Yohai said, "Great is peace for all blessings and prayers conclude with an invocation for peace. In the case of the reading of *Shema*, the prayers in that section of the service end with: "We praise You, O God, may your sheltering peace descend"; in the case of the *Tefillah*, the final prayer in that section of the service is, "We praise You, O God, the source of peace"; in the case of the Priestly Benediction, one concludes, "May God reach out to You in tenderness, and give you peace."[35]

The wars commanded in the Torah, the fighting against the Jebusites, the Perrizites, Hitites and others were categorized by our Rabbis in the Mishnah, 2000 years ago, as something entirely exceptional, *milchemet mitzvah*, uniquely commanded wars, not to be repeated.[36] These Rabbis were suffering from the results of the Jewish revolt of 66 CE and the Hadrianic revolt of 135 CE. Both were started by zealots saying that they were doing so for a holy cause, and both had devastating consequences for Jews and Judaism.

---

[32] Deuteronomy 9:1ff
[33] Isaiah 2:2
[34] Isaiah 11:9
[35] Leviticus Rabbah 9:9, quoting Numbers 6:26
[36] Mishnah Sotah 8:7

But there is a small section of the Jewish people who are trying to revive the idea that there can be a war for Jews which is a religious obligation. The war, and it may now be accurately called a war between Israel and the Palestinians, is defined by many religiously observant settlers and their supporters as a divine obligation to reclaim the whole of the Land of Israel as either a prelude to, or as actually part of, the messianic awakening. They base this on a statement of Nachmanides from the twelfth century.[37]

When they do this, Jewish warmongers are on the level of the chimpanzees of the Ugandan National Park, with disastrous consequences for the society around them, making it impossible for Israel to find the just and secure peace that we all need.

Today's Jews in the Diaspora and Israel need to pursue that essential direction of Judaism towards peace and away from violence. How should we do so? Rabbi Tony Bayfield wrote in *Manna* that there are six points to pursuing peace in Israel for we Diaspora Jews. We must love Israel no less than those who would have her be a war-mongering state. We should state that our commitment to Israel is to a just and secure peace based on two states, not some apparent biblical claim which our Rabbis told us was finished two thousand years ago. We must proudly share with Israel the value of the Diaspora perspective, because "the future of the Jewish people worldwide is bound up both ethically and physically with the future of the Jewish people in Israel." Therefore we must contribute to Israel and pass on the understanding of how people outside Israel see the situation she is in. We must engage in the important work of building alliances and partnerships with everyone working in Israel and the Middle East so that we can get through challenges together when they occur. If we work with those with a different perspective, then we can get our perspective across. When the Methodist Church worked on

---

[37] In his gloss on Maimonides' *Book of Commandments* (positive commandment 4), which teaches that the conquest and settlement of the Land of Israel lies in the category of obligatory war (*milhemet mitzvah*). "It is a positive commandment for all generations obligating every individual, even during the period of exile".

projects to alleviate poverty among Middle Eastern Christians they did so without the perspective of the prosperity that Israel could bring to the region. Finally, we must urge Israel to enshrine in law and practice the pursuit of justice and the principle of equality for all peoples.[38]

We must raise ourselves and help to raise Israel so that in her peace we too will have peace. And we must not be scared to call those who try to build Israel through caring nothing for the needs of her non-Jewish citizens and neighbours effectively anti-Zionist. For their version of Zionism will just send us the way of the violent chimpanzees.

---

[38] *Manna*, Summer 2010, p1

# How Faiths Invest Their Assets

ANYONE WHO HAS travelled to the United States of America and is not a US citizen will know what a royal pain the US immigration procedures are. First there are these complicated forms to fill in even if you are only staying there for a couple of days. Then, having left an aeroplane in which you have been cooped up for many hours you are again cooped up in a long snake of a line on the ground – waiting for your turn to be called to the two or three boxes open out of ten or so in the arrivals hall. Once, in the days before the ESTA, the more rapid Electronic System for Travel Authorisation, it took me a good hour to get from the door of the plane to the baggage hall in Washington DC. I had filled out the form on the plane like a good citizen so as not to hold up the queues, I had ticked all the boxes correctly and written my details box by box in clear block letters. So I had quite a lot of queuing time to do and I began to wonder. On the card there are a number of personal declarations that you are meant to make.

One is, "Are you seeking entry to the US to engage in criminal or immoral activities?" You will be pleased to know that I ticked the *no* box, but whoever ticks the *yes* box? Is there anybody in the whole world so clueless as to approach the immigration officer having declared their intention to engage in criminal acts and then to say, "Oh it's OK it'll just be a little pickpocketing, and I plan to overstay on parking meters", to which the immigration officer replies, I guess, "Sorry, I can't give you a ninety-day visa but you can come in for thirty days on our special petty larceny tourism scheme."

The next question on the form is one to which I suspect it is even less likely to get an honest answer from would-be entrants to the US. It is this: "Have you ever been or are you now involved in espionage or sabotage or in terrorist activities?" Now I don't know for sure, but I would imagine that in basic training to be a spy or a member of a terrorist network you learn never to tell a government official of your enemy nation that you plan to spy on or attack their country. So I don't imagine the US immigration officials often see a tick in the *yes* box for that one.

One more question on the form which obviously has praiseworthy intentions but which also, I would imagine, rarely if ever elicits a truthful response from those to whom it applies, is this one: "Between 1933 and 1945 were you involved in any way in persecutions associated with Nazi Germany or its allies?" Can't imagine that that question is the most effective way of ensuring that the US does not harbour Nazis!

The fact is that if you did tick *yes* to any of those questions there would be inevitable consequences of your saying just the wrong thing at the wrong time.

It was an attempt to do the right thing at the right time that led me to Washington that time. The issue is this. It is businesses that wield real power in our world: of the 100 largest economies in the world 51 are corporations and 49 are nation states. These businesses have power to improve or damage our environment, power to make the lives of billions fulfilling, with a living wage, or to leave them destitute, power to encourage or discourage cultures of corruption among government officials. Power really to shape our world is in the hands of businesses. Some businesses, some of the time, do not use this power properly, only being concerned with the financial bottom line of their activities and not the social or environmental consequences of their actions. Some turn a blind eye to the existence and conditions of child labour among the subcontractors that they use, give donations to prop up corrupt regimes which they feel will give their business activities a stable environment in which to operate whilst the people are oppressed, some contribute excessively to pollution so that they make money whilst our environment suffers. There are also businesses which take their triple bottom line seriously, aware that their success in the long-term depends upon favourable social and environmental conditions, so that the number and wealth of consumers increases worldwide and the resources of the world are preserved for the use of all.

The religions and uniting philosophies of the world, Judaism, Christianity, Islam, Hindu, Jainism, Sikhism, Zoroastrianism, Shinto and Buddhism, share some values which comment on the conduct of business. They all aim for their followers at least, and, for most faiths, all the peoples of the world to live full lives, unexploited by each other. They all hope to see grinding poverty relieved. Also all of these religions see the Earth as worthy of our care and stewardship for future generations.

Their creed would then ask a certain standard of behaviour from businesses. From their pulpits they preach social justice and care of the world. But who owns the large businesses of the world? For the most part we do – through our pension funds (in Britain over 40% of the entire value of the companies in the stock market is owned by pension funds), through individual share ownership, through the holdings in them by institutions we support. All the religions that I mentioned have between them a membership of two-thirds of the entire population of the world, some richer, some poorer, but all sharing a belief in social justice and stewardship of the Earth and all affected by the actions of businesses.

I was in Washington DC to attend a conference of the International Interfaith Investment Group (3iG), which I serve on their Executive Committee. 3iG asks the religions of the world to examine their own portfolio of investments and to make sure that they are invested in businesses whose activities are not at odds with their own tenets, and also which turn into reality the positive values of those religions.

In a 2010 meeting, for example, we heard about new investment opportunities, enabling faith groups to put their values into direct action through investing a proportion of their assets in something very positive. We heard from the World Bank, who were marketing bonds which will enable them to finance immunization programmes in developing countries. We heard from a group selling investments, backed by many large foundations, in public transport infrastructure in developing world capital cities. We heard from a Church of Sweden diocese which set up a business in Mozambique re-foresting and harvesting thousands of acres of depleted land, in co-operation with local people. We heard from a Geneva-based bank which exists to make loans to people in the poorest parts of the world and who can otherwise have no access to capital. Their average loan to people in the poorest areas of South America and Africa is only $260 dollars, but people are starting successful businesses on this money and pulling themselves out of poverty, and you and I can invest in this and get a return. The 3iG delegates heard about an investment offered by a trust in the gum arabic industry in Darfur. They were looking for international investors in improving the water infrastructure which will enable Christian and Muslim Darfuris together to improve their lot through trade with the big food companies of the world. This natural product of the acacia tree is used in virtually every artificially made drink and food. Why invest? Because the return that a religious investor will get is a financial benefit, they will be helping to create an environmentally sustainable industry in Darfur and, most importantly, the terrible ethnic strife will surely reduce in the long term if there is more wealth in the Darfur region.

What would make 3iG a real force for good in the world would be if the idea of investing not just for financial return but also for social and environmental return spread from the religious institutions to the congregants of those institutions, so that for all of us we reduce the dissonance between our beliefs and our investments. It would be a *Kiddush HaShem*, an honouring of God with our wealth, the opposite of the *Hillul HaShem* of blasphemy and bad business practice.

The Torah tells us not to do our everyday work on Shabbat. But note the word that is used for work in Exodus is *m'lachah*, not the regular modern Hebrew word for work, which is *avodah*.[39] The word *avodah* is from the

---

[39] Leviticus 23:3

27

same Hebrew root as *eved*, which means servant or slave. For sure there are times when work feels just like that, being under another person's control, not being free to do what we would with our time. But *m'lachah* means work too. It is related to the Hebrew root *melech*, which means king or ruler, and that also is what our work is about. It is our opportunity to create something new, to gain some mastery over the world, it is where we make our greatest contribution to the world. So if we must stop our work on Shabbat, for the other days of the week we should be using our work to serve others but also for making our contribution to a better world. We can put our investments to work for us if we ensure that as well as giving us the return that we need, they are working for us to sustain a world that a Jew, or a Christian or a Muslim or a Buddhist or any of the peoples of the world would want to live in, both in terms of what we don't invest in and what we do invest in.

# Kiddush HaShem

SIMEON BEN GAMLIEL, Ishmael the High Priest, Akiva ben Joseph, Chananiah ben Teradion, Chutzpit the Interpreter, Elazar ben Shemua, Chanina ben Chakinai, Yeshevav the Scribe, Judah ben Damah, Judah ben Bava. Names to strike fear into the person who each year has the *mitzvah* of reading them out on Yom Kippur during the Musaf Service, when we reach the section of the service called the Matryology or *Eleh Ezkerah*.

Capital punishment was part of the judicial systems of the Middle East during the times of our Bible, and remains so now. The deaths of the ten teachers of Torah are commemorated in the Yom Kippur service because of their martyrdom. They are called to mind because they were part of a distinguished but horrendous chain of martyrdom which has accompanied the history of Judaism right up to the present day.

Martyrdom in Judaism is known by a surprising phrase given the evil which has caused it to be necessary, *Kiddush HaShem* (the sanctification of God's name). This term is derived from a verse in Leviticus in a section which deals with a number of aspects of sanctification: the holiness of the priests, the holiness of the festival days, the holiness of the place in which they were celebrated, and the holiness of God's name. "You must not profane My holy name so that I may be sanctified in the midst of the Israelite people, I am the Eternal One who sanctifies you."[40] As the festivals and Shabbatot of the Jewish year aim to sanctify God in time and the priests aimed to sanctify God in their ritual, so should our actions aim to sanctify God in deed.

The Rabbis reasoned that there was no clearer way of showing how special and holy God was to you than to die for your religion, hence the word for this ultimate deed became *Kiddush HaShem*, the sanctification of God's

---

[40] Leviticus 22:32

name. At no point, though, has mainstream Judaism seen it as acceptable for a person to seek martyrdom, and so in Judaism a person who committed homicide by killing civilians and blowing themselves up in the process would not be called a martyr but rather a murderer.

Jewish martyrdom, *Kiddush HaShem,* has continued up until the present day. There are, for example, many instances in the Shoah, the Holocaust, of people who laid down their lives for their right to continue to practice their Judaism, or simply because they were considered to be Jewish by the Nazis' racial laws. In our service for Yom Ha Shoah our memorial prayer, *El Male Rachamim*, says directly that the victims of the Shoah died for *Kiddush HaShem.* But, thank God, it is inconceivable that we today will ever be required to make that choice. Does that then mean that *Kiddush HaShem*, the sanctification of God's name, is something that we cannot do unless we are forced into it by oppressors and persecutors?

Not at all. It is something that we could do every day. Some Jews attempt to sanctify God's name by using it in all of their daily correspondence. You may have seen at the top of Bar Mitzvah invitations printed by Orthodox printers and at the top of letters written by observant Jews the letters *Bet* and *Heh* separated by what look like quotation marks. These letters stand for the Hebrew words *B'ezrat HaShem*, with the help of the holy Name. Those who use this convention are suggesting that God is intimately bound up in every action which they take.

Even the singer Dana International, the Israeli winner of the Eurovision song contest in 1998, performed a minor act of *Kiddush HaShem* when, as she was quoted in the *Jewish Chronicle*, she said that she felt that, "I knew God was with me. This is the proof that we are all equal in God's eyes." By bringing the name of God into such a major achievement in her life she brought people's attention to the encouragement that a Jewish religious outlook can give us.

As unlikely that it is, thank God, that we will find ourselves in a position where martyrdom is the only honourable option, so it is unlikely that any of us will win the Eurovision song contest. Yet we do not need to make statements before the whole public or the whole Jewish people to succeed in sanctifying God's name, to do *Kiddush HaShem*. We can do so in very many aspects of our daily life.

How so? In the Babylonian Talmud there features a discussion of what constitutes *Kiddush HaShem* which ends with these words: "You [as a Jew] should cause God to be loved through your acts. So if a person studies Judaism and is honest in his business dealings and speaks gently to people, what do people say about him? 'Happy are the parents who taught him Torah. Happy is the teacher who taught him Torah. This person studied Torah and see how noble his ways are, how good his actions.' But when a person studies Judaism yet is dishonest in business and is rude and abusive to people, what do people say of him? 'Woe unto him who studies Torah ... this man studied Torah; look how corrupt are his deeds, how ugly his ways.'"[41]

It is profanation of God's name, almost blasphemy, to do your duty by studying Judaism and then go out and be bad to other people in business or simply in your social relations. It is sanctification of God's name, *Kiddush HaShem*, to be guided by your Jewish religion and learning to be honest and upright and pleasant to the people whom you encounter.

Another interpretation of the meaning of *Kiddush HaShem*, in the days when Jews lived under constant threat of massacre, during the Crusades, was provided by Rabbi Moshe of Coucy in France. You might have thought during those troubled times that no further demands should be put on Jews than just to keep to their faith, but Rabbi Moshe was still able to maintain that Jews must sanctify God's name by their own good behaviour. Martyrdom would only be the most extreme example. He wrote: "Jews must ... not lie to a Jew or non-Jew, and not mislead anyone in any matter ... For if Jews cheat non-Jews, they will say, 'Look how God chose for His people a nation of thieves and deceivers' ... Indeed God dispersed us among

---

[41] Babylonian Talmud Yoma 86a

the nations so that we could gather converts to Judaism, but if we behave deceitfully towards others who will want to join us?"[42]

In our day it is not only how we behave as Jews that is at issue if we wish to sanctify God's name. In our society we are not always recognisable as Jews and I would therefore add to the hierarchy of *Kiddush HaShem* the desirability of making it clear that we are proud to be who we are. We have several ways we can do this – one of the most simple, direct, and indeed one which is explicitly commanded in the Torah is to be confident enough of our own identity and our wish to bear witness to God in the Jewish way, to place on the outside doorpost of our homes the mezuzah. I am often surprised when I visit homes in our community and there is no mezuzah outside. The people inside the houses are by no means ashamed of their Judaism and there is no doubt for me that their Judaism is encouraging them to lead good lives. Why do they not wish to tell their neighbours who they are?

Then there is at work and at college and school. For example, what should a person do if they have just started at a new college or a new employer when Rosh Hashanah or Yom Kippur come around? To me it seems obvious, it is *Kiddush HaShem*, the sanctification of God's name, to make it clear immediately that you are a Jew and will always need these special days off. Is it far off *Hilul HaShem*, the profanation of God's name, either not to reveal your Jewish identity or to make it appear to your employer or tutors that your Judaism means too little to you to absent yourself on those days? That may not be the way you feel it, but surely that is how it looks to others.

I believe that there is a further *Kiddush HaShem* that we can do. That is voting and doing so in a way which gives political expression to our religious values. Rabbi Jonathan Romain notes that one of Hillel's first principles of Judaism is that we must never separate ourselves from the

---

[42] Quoted in *Jewish Wisdom*, ed. Joseph Telushkin (New York: William Morrow, 1994), pp318-319

community around us and that where there are no people of visionary courage each Jew must try to fulfil that role themselves.[43] The prophet Amos says that God needs us to work with Him to "Let justice roll down like water and righteousness like an everlasting stream."[44] This means that we should be seeking to vote for the party which we feel will best protect vulnerable groups in society, enable Israel to thrive and come ever closer to peace with her neighbours, uphold human rights, respond to the needs of the stranger, work for peace and build a society where everyone can reach their best potential, as is the Jewish mission in this world.

Involvement in politics for the sake of God's name has been mandated for Jews ever since the prophet Jeremiah said, "Pray to God for the peace of the city within which you live for in its peace you will find your peace."[45] Political apathy is not an option for a Jew who wants to do *Kiddush HaShem*, whoever you vote for!

---

[43] Mishnah Avot 2:5-6
[44] Amos 5:24
[45] Jeremiah 29:7

# Jewish Global Concern

# The Ocean Is A Wilderness

ON 13ᵀᴴ MAY 1939, 930 German-Jewish refugees boarded the Hamburg-Amerika Line's "St Louis" with Cuban landing permissions. They set sail from Hamburg with 10 Reichmarks each and a suitcase, having had to surrender all their other assets. In the face of adverse comment of an antisemitic nature in the local press the Cuban government revoked the landing permissions. The United States refused to take the refugees even though 734 of them had quota numbers to enter the USA as immigrants.

The ship was turned round to return to Europe and docked in Antwerp where 287 of the passengers were granted permission to enter Britain, 244 to France, 214 to Belgium and 181 to Holland, thanks to the efforts of the Joint Distribution Committee. Of course many of those who went to countries which were later taken over by the Nazis did not survive the Shoah.

Although Britain was third only to the United States and Argentina in the number of refugees that she saved from death, taking in 52,000 Jews, the *Daily Express*, in its editorial on the issue on 19th June 1939, was less than charitable, saying, "The plight of these refugees wandering helplessly over the seas searching in search of a home won the sympathy of the world. The decision to allow some of them to land in this country was approved by public opinion. This example must not set a precedent. There is no room for any more refugees in this country."

In July 1947, a passenger ship destined for Palestine and named the "Exodus" was stopped and boarded by the British Navy. The ship was crowded with Shoah survivors determined to make a new life for themselves in British-controlled Palestine. The British, facing Zionist resistance and trying to keep promises made to the Palestinian Arabs to limit Jewish immigration, were determined to stop it. Accordingly, when the Royal Navy boarded the ship twenty miles out from Haifa, a full-scale battle ensued.

Three migrants were killed and dozens injured as British troops beat the passengers on to three separate prison ships. From there these Shoah survivors were transported back to Germany and were once again placed in camps.

The world was horrified; an American newspaper ran the headline, "Back to the Reich". Delegates from the UN Special Commission on Palestine who watched what occurred were similarly shocked; the Yugoslav delegate cited that what happened to the "Exodus", "is the best possible evidence we have for allowing Jews into Palestine".

Since then, the fate of the "Exodus" has achieved legendary status: Leon Uris used it as the basis for his 1958 bestseller of the same name, an award-winning film starring Paul Newman came out in 1960, and the former Israeli foreign minister, Abba Eban, drew a direct link between the "Exodus" story and the ending of British rule in Palestine.

The ocean is a wilderness on which you set sail at your peril if you do not have a destination ready to accept you. The Jewish people have known this experience and we share our history down our generations.

It should drive us to empathise with the multitude who take to boats on the shores of North Africa in the hope of reaching asylum in Europe, or from Myanmar and Bangladesh in the hope of dignity and human rights in Malaysia or Indonesia. The danger they face is staggering. In 2015, in the Mediterranean alone, nearly two thousand would-be migrants are known to have drowned as their boats failed.

Throughout the year there are hundreds if not thousands of people crammed into boats on the Mediterranean and the Andaman Sea, trying like our people did in the past to cross the wilderness, not the land but the sea, and not on their own but under the control of people who have charged them impossible amounts of money for the rudimentary equipment to attempt the crossing.

People do make it. According to the United Nations, 200,000 migrants entered the European Union following a sea crossing of the Mediterranean in 2014. They come from Syria, Eritrea, Sudan, repressive countries where violence, disrespect for human rights and economic disaster create conditions in which none of us would want to raise our families. In Judaism we cannot just see them as people who are not us and thus beyond our care. Rather, every person counts and we must empathise with their situation.

In doing so we do something quintessentially Jewish which reaches into the very heart of Jewish theology and mysticism. We start with the way that Judaism thinks of creation. As the Reform Judaism theologian, Eugene Borowitz, puts it, in Christian society, and also for many Jews who grow up in that milieu, "creation is usually thought of in spatial terms and is seen as a moment of externalisation. That is, God puts the creation 'out there'."

"Think of the ceiling of the Vatican City's Sistine Chapel. Michelangelo pictured God as a mighty muscular hand stretching full length to one fingertip and bringing Adam into being."[46] God, as it were, extends into our world to bring it into being. God at the top, humanity down below.

Rabbi Isaac Luria in sixteenth-century Safed felt otherwise. If God is everywhere, he reasoned, there is no "out there" in which to put creation. In order to create anything, God must first contract. God, said Luria, creates by pulling back. Luria called this act *tzimtzum.* God's *tzimtzum* leaves a void that enables God's creatures to have a space in which to come into being.

---

[46] Eugene Borowitz, *A Touch of the Sacred* (Woodstock: Jewish Lights, 2009), pp71-72

But when God withdrew He left behind, in the space in which we come to be, a residue of God's reality, "like the little bit of oil left when we think the jug is fully empty". Luria's Kabbalah calls this residue "remaining beams of God's creative light", once contained in vessels so that we could behold them but too strong for the vessels to contain. So they shattered, the process that Luria calls *sh'virah.* The problem with our world is that we live among the shells or husks of what might have been. Yet some sparks of God's energizing light remain.

This is why every one of us counts. In the opening chapters of the Book of Numbers each Israelite was individually counted.[47] If every bit of God's divine sparks could mystically be restored to their proper place in God's being then all things would become as they were intended to be. Through human acts of *tikkun olam,* which literally means "repair or restoration of the world", God's wholeness of creation would appear. Luria understood our task in *tikkun olam* to be following the Torah in its full mystic depth.

This means that humanity has the power to bring the Messianic Age, to heal the world, piece by broken piece. Every single one of us has our contribution to make to this healing. No king, or queen, or president is any more responsible than you or me. We may each have a task suiting our talents and skills, but none of us can defer to another person we think greater than us to do it.

You can see this illustrated clearly in so many places in Judaism. For community prayer to begin we need a *minyan,* ten people to make it communal. In the Altneuschul in Prague, the oldest synagogue in Europe, there is a jail cell attached to the shul which was used for miscreants in the community. This cell has a porthole open to the synagogue so that the man in the jail could be counted in the minyan for the services in the synagogue. Everyone counts. When you are called up to Torah you are called up by name as each of us has a name and an identity. Each of us counts individually.

---

[47] Numbers 1:20ff

In God's eyes, as it should be in our own, we are individuals with a sacred task to participate in repairing the world in our lifetime, if at all possible. So no Jew should ever despise another person, no Jew should ever act as if someone who is different from them does not count. We must always find and support the potential in each other because the person we are facing may just hold the key to one of those sparks of God's light which must be restored to its proper place.

So we cannot wish away the plight of the boat people of our day. We need to encourage our government to join with the others of Europe and, through the United Nations, the world. People in danger of drowning must be rescued. A humane system of processing the claims of those who have a refugee's right to asylum, perhaps through camps in North Africa and Lebanon, which are outposts of potential receiving countries, should be set up so that you don't need to set out into the dangerous seas to have your case heard.

In our hearts we should place ourselves alongside the desperate people in those boats, knowing that in their lives was once our people's experience too. We pray that they will find safety and security as we wish for ourselves.

# Don't Panic! This World May Be An Experiment

UP TO A few years ago, on the back of the booklet which explained the Bar and Bat Mitzvah process at our synagogue, we used to print the words, "Don't Panic". We don't use these words any more, not because people should begin to panic about this life-cycle ceremony, but because time has passed and not so many people remember what it is referring to. They came from the words on the back of a fictional book called *The Hitchhiker's Guide to the Galaxy*.

*The Hitchhiker's Guide to the Galaxy* series by Douglas Adams began as a radio show on Radio 4, then became a series of books, a television series and a film, all set in imaginary worlds where strange but ultimately logical things happened. For example, *The Hitchhiker's Guide to the Galaxy* introduced us to the restaurant at the end of the universe, Milliways, whose astronomical prices could be afforded by anyone as long as they deposited a single penny in an interest-bearing bank account in their own time. The effect of compound interest on this penny deposit would be that, when a method of time travel became available to enable the depositor to reach the very end of time, they would be so wealthy that they could afford to eat at the restaurant.

Behind the series was the search for the ultimate meaning of life, the universe and everything. In the first book of *The Hitchhiker's Guide* series they come up with the answer to the ultimate question of life, the universe and everything, which I shall not reveal here. But then the protagonists realise that they were never sure what the question itself was. That, according to *The Hitchhiker's Guide to the Galaxy,* is why the Earth exists.

It exists as a scientific experiment running for a number of billions of years in order to find the meaning of life, the universe and everything. This experiment is being carried out and monitored by the mice. These are the same mice that we think we are observing in our experimentation, but in fact the mice are actually observing us on behalf of the other citizens of the universe. Far-fetched? Of course, that is the luxury of science fiction.

Science fiction it might be, yet this particular idea of the world as an experiment is one which exists in our Midrash. When we hear the first chapter of Genesis the word *tov,* good, appears many times. It occurs as God's assessment of each day of creation according to the Torah account, except for one. On the sixth and last day of active creation, in which the land animals and Adam, the man-and-woman of Genesis chapter 1, are created, we hear that, "God saw everything that he had created and found it *tov me'od,* very good."[48]

Very good in comparison to what? In comparison to the birds, sea creatures, land, seas, Earth, Moon and Sun? Surely not! Who is to say that a parrot fish is good, but a ring tailed lemur is very good, just because it figures in the Torah's account of the sixth day whilst the fish appears on day five? Who is to say that a condor is good, but a vole is very good, because the condor was created on day five and the vole on day six?

So Rabbi Abbahu said *no.* The comparison made was that this world which we inhabit and which the Torah seeks to instruct us about was very good compared to all of the others which God had previously created and destroyed in His attempt to create the perfect Earth.[49] This would be of little consequence to we who are searching for a lesson from our legend of creation except that we have to note that the world was just "very good" at the end of creation. For those who currently receive school reports, or reports from your employer or who remember these, you will sympathise that "very good" isn't great. It is not excellent, it is not superb, it is certainly not perfect. The Midrash suggests that this world too, our world, is also an experiment. It is not the perfect one. But

---

[48] Genesis 1:31
[49] Bereshit Rabbah 3:7

that then establishes the mission of Judaism and of all human effort to make it so.

When Adam is created in the Torah account he is not called good nor very good, rather he is covered by the "very good" that sums up the whole of the world on the sixth day of creation. Light was good, land and sea were good, the flora were good, the sun and moon were good, the sea creatures and birds and reptiles were good, but not humanity. This inconsistency was picked up in the Talmud to add further understanding to the concept of free will, which is crucial to Judaism.[50] In Judaism man is not good by nature or he would been called such in the Torah account of his creation. But neither is he bad by nature or he would have been called such in the Torah account of his creation.

Rather, in Judaism, man and woman can go any way reacting to their *yetzer hatov,* their inclination to do good, and their *yetzer hara,* inclination to do evil. It is the free choice of each of us which way we go, there is no such thing as personal destiny in Judaism. Cain showed this when he made the choice to allow jealousy to get the better of him and he murdered his brother. God in the story as it is presented in the Torah is no less surprised and disgusted by Cain's actions than we the readers are meant to be. There is no suggestion in the Torah that this evil was Cain's destiny.[51]

Whilst there is no such thing as personal destiny in Judaism, there is such a thing as a communal destiny. It is made explicit in the Books of the Prophets. We are charged by Isaiah, communicating what were to him the words of the Almighty, "I created you to be a light to the nations."[52] Our destiny as the Jewish people was and remains to be among those who bring the world closer to perfection. Zechariah paints a picture of a world where by being kind, compassionate, just and true with each other we bring about a world closer to perfection, to redemption in a Messianic

---

[50] Babylonian Talmud Berachot 61a
[51] Genesis Chapter 4
[52] Isaiah 49:6

Age of peace and harmony.[53] This message, repeated again and again in the Haftarot that we hear every Shabbat, is not only to do with relationships between people, nor our own relationship with God, but also harks back to the sixth day of creation.

On that sixth day all the land animals and man were created. Also on the sixth day man was given dominion over creation and he was given the produce of the earth to be his food. It was at that point that God saw all that he had made and found it to be very good. Meaning that, with all working in harmony with each other, the world achieved the status of very good. When man's ability to alter the course of nature is held in check with responsibility then it is very good. When man's needs for food, clothing and material prosperity preserves and develops the good of the Earth rather than simply consuming with a voracious appetite what is there until it is all gone, then it is very good. Humanity seems far from very good at the moment, with an area of rainforest the size of Great Britain destroyed every year; with, to give just one more example, the sixty million bison of pre-revolutionary America reduced to just a few thousand in one hundred years. We are not managing our part of "very good".

Every generation leaves the world knowing that it has not yet managed to bring the world to being "very good". It means that it is our responsibility to pass on the principles and ethical mechanisms which will enable future generations to take it even further towards perfection. We have to teach each succeeding generation the correct answer to Cain's question, "Am I my brother's keeper?"[54] The answer *no* is not the right answer. Lack of responsibility for others means degradation for all. Saying that the world is God's responsibility is also wrong because we are not handed a perfect world, but one which is perfectible or degradable by our actions. The right answer is *yes*. We are responsible for guarding the world and each other.

---

[53] E.g. Zechariah 8:16
[54] Genesis 4:9

# Please, No Plastic Fruit In Our Sukkah

THERE IS A man in our congregation, now in his nineties, who admits to not having always been the upstanding citizen that he is today. He was brought up in the East End of London and when he was a young boy he and his friends used to be what was called in the Yiddish of the day *lobboses*. His favourite example of this comes from the festival of Sukkot, the Jewish harvest festival. On the festival, just as today, observant Jews build a Sukkah somewhere outside on their property. As long as the sky can be seen through the roof, elaborate or simple, made in wood or other material and covered in leaves, flowers and fruit, they symbolise the makeshift shelters of the Israelites as refugees from Egyptian slavery, wandering across the desert, and they celebrate the harvest of the year by their decoration.

With all of these Sukkahs in people's back yards in the part of the East End where our friend was brought up, the temptation was rather too great for him and his *lobbos* friends. The fruit that hangs down from the roof of a well-made Sukkah was very attractive to boys in the Great Depression era early 1930s. So he has to admit that they were delighted when Sukkot came along and, by scaling up back-yard walls and other acts of derring-do, he and his friends were able to pinch an apple or two, or even a coveted orange from the orange groves of Jaffa in Mandate Palestine, from the Sukkah decorations, and scoff them in the alleyway. One particular Sukkah was always especially well-endowed with fruit each year and was a year-by-year target for the boys. That was until the year when the owner wised up to what was happening. Our congregant and his friends dropped down over the wall to discover to their horror that this year all of the fruit hanging down had been replaced by turnips, onions and carrots!

When I grew up, the smell, the feel and the look of a Sukkah was always dominated by the freshness of nature. At Wembley Liberal Synagogue, the presence of the Sukkah pervaded the whole building, as it was built in a side room to the synagogue that had a skylight. People brought greenery from their gardens, and we decorated the Sukkah with fruits which, after Sukkot, were then, in those less health-and-safety-conscious days, given to our local Jewish old-age home.

It was the same at my first pulpit, Woodford Progressive Synagogue. The Sukkah was also inside the building, right beside the *Bimah* in fact, and pervaded the whole sanctuary with its presence, reminding us of the nature celebration roots of the festival. During my time there we came to move it outside to the synagogue courtyard to enhance its kashrut, and now it provides a yearly Jewish landmark on the road where the synagogue stands.

At our synagogue our Sukkah is put up by a large gang of volunteers and decorated by a hundred or more adults and children together. Most of the laurel that makes its roof is grown on the synagogue grounds, the rest comes from the garden of a member. The flowers are those from our tent on Yom Kippur, which we erect to accommodate a congregation of nearly two thousand, given a new lease of life outside. The fruit is brought by our children to our religious school on Sunday then hung, together with a whole box of apples from one garden and grapes grown in several others, and finally quite a bit of fruit bought specially for decorating. The decorated CDs glinting in the sun are an inspired idea for what to do with the mountain of blank CDs left over from the days before Cloud IT storage, when they were the way we kept data.

This UK kind of Sukkah is not the way a Sukkah looks in the rest of the world. In the Southern Hemisphere most local fruit is out of season at this time of the year, so in South Africa and Australia many decorate their Sukkah with pictures of the fruits of God's earth, drawn by children. That was what I encountered to my surprise when I arrived in Cape Town on Sukkot, where of course it was the tail end of winter, not of summer, as it is in the U.K. In Israel many *marpeset* (balcony) Sukkahs are decorated with what seem pretty obviously to the British eye to be

Christmas decorations. Apparently the baubles and tinsel that Britain associates with Christmas are especially popular for Sukkahs in ultra-orthodox Mea Shearim. And indeed if a family asks me if it's OK to have a Christmas tree I suggest to them that rather than making this tradition to commemorate a Christian festival as an aspect of family togetherness, build a Sukkah together instead. A Sukkah gives more decorative scope than a single tree and you can eat your meals in it!

One of the enjoyable aspects of building a Sukkah is that you chat to the people you are doing it with. It's one of the things I love about Sukkah-building morning here at the synagogue, as parents who barely know each other talk as they bravely scale ladders and hack at the synagogue's laurel with secateurs. In Britain and in a synagogue which extends a welcome to refugees new to the country, one theme of conversation has stood out. Basically and simply, what on earth are we doing? Hanging up perfectly good fruit as decoration rather than giving it away. A few of our Sukkah decorators have suggested that the synagogue Sukkah should rather be decorated with plastic fruit that can be reused from year to year.

I feel a visceral reaction to this suggestion. No! Surely handling, preparing, hanging and seeing the real thing is central to the British experience of Sukkot. Please, no plastic fruit.

Why do I feel so strongly? Is this just because of my childhood experience of Sukkot? Is it because of the risk of the East End story of the apples and turnips becoming meaningless for our next generations? Perhaps. But more so, I am convinced that we need real fruit and greenery on our Sukkah for reasons that are the face-value meaning of the Torah portions that we read over Sukkot. On the festival itself our Torah portion sets up Sukkot as not only the remembrance of the flimsy shelters of the Exodus but also the time of celebration of the harvest, indeed we are commanded to celebrate and be joyful at this time.[55] We city-dwelling Jews are far

---

[55] Leviticus 23:39ff

removed from harvests. When we want to eat there are shops everywhere stocked up and ready to serve us.

It is very easy and natural to take this for granted, so the fruits in the Sukkah remind us that our lives are in the hands of the productivity of the earth. We live with food security in London, yet every day in this country, which imports over 40% of its food, we are at all times only a few days away from shortage if there were to be a blockage to distribution channels, and a few weeks from troubles if there were to be widespread blights. In sub-Saharan Africa the effects can be very rapid. Drought in Zimbabwe in 2015 meant that the maize harvest was less than 50% of the norm, leaving more than 1.5 million people dependent on food aid to avoid starvation.[56] Sukkot connects us with the global harvest. Though you may see a banana hanging from our Sukkah and ask what does that have to do with our harvest here, it reminds us that for us in London food is a global issue.

Our well-being is a partnership between us, God, nature and the rest of the peoples of the world. It is built on the good decisions of previous generations, who ensured that we can eat and be satisfied because of the way they farmed the land. It is built on the continued willingness of the rest of the world to supply us with food. It is built on God-given rains and sun without which any year could be a food disaster. It will be sustained by our care for the environment. Not only should we care, but we also need other countries to care. We know that this requires us to make choices which use less energy, which clear less of the rainforest, which reduce air pollution and the resulting greenhouse gases. The act of properly building a Sukkah, making us think about what we decorate it with and using sustainable biodegradable fruits seems just right to link us with these questions.

I hope that our synagogue Sukkah remains fully natural, to me the real thing. I hope that it remains elemental and properly linked with the

---

[56] *The Economist*, 3 October 2015, p54

47

harvests which we need to survive. You can make a lovely Sukkah out of plastic but it will remind you only of our spiritual historical narrative and not our current inter-connectedness with nature. We could cut the food miles by only hanging fruits which were grown locally, in members' gardens, and perhaps to do that we could plant some fruit trees here in our synagogue garden. But let's ensure that our celebration of Sukkot is as multifaceted as it was always intended to be.

# Degrees Of Charity In The Twenty-First Century

TWO BEGGARS WERE sitting on the pavement just outside the Vatican. One was holding a large cross and the other a large Magen David, the Jewish symbol of the Star of David. Both were holding out their hats to collect contributions. As people walked by virtually none of them put any money in the hat of the man holding the Magen David but the hat of the man holding the cross was virtually full to the brim in no time.

A kindly priest on pilgrimage to Rome watched for a while with a heavy heart and then approached the men. With eyes full of concern he turned to the man with the Magen David and said, "The Vatican is such an important site to Christians. I am so sorry, but you will never get any contributions holding a Star of David."

The man holding the Magen David turned to the man holding the cross and said, "Moishe, look who's trying to teach us marketing."

We have been advised many times by those agencies and charities which should know what they are talking about that we would do better not to give loose change and little bits of money to the beggars who are so prevalent on the streets of London nowadays. These charities and agencies tell us that if we really want to help those in need on the streets of London then we should make a regular or one-off donation to Shelter, Centrepoint, the Refugee Council, local housing action campaigns for the homeless or similar welfare groups. Only they can ensure that your money is going to a person in genuine need for worthwhile purposes.

Even so, and even though over the past decade or so since the English taboo against begging has pretty much broken down, there are now so many beggars that it becomes necessary to become inured to them. Occasionally I suspect that most of us once in a while feel compelled to give to one person who approaches us at the right time in the right way. I know I do.

Our Torah and Talmud and pretty much all subsequent Jewish sources have always considered giving charity in whatever circumstances to be a *mitzvah*, an obligation upon a Jew. Of course earlier Jewish sources mostly portray charity as something done between one person and another directly, there having been no government housing agencies or NGOs two thousand years ago. Charity was a transaction between the beggar and the giver.

We are used to the idea that the beggar should be appreciative when given our coppers, but Judaism would have it just the other way, that the giver should thank the beggar for asking him or her. By responding, the giver has been given the opportunity to do a *mitzvah,* to fulfil a Jewish duty, at very little cost or inconvenience to himself. Once Rabbi Bunam was asked why there is no blessing when giving charity as there is when performing other *mitzvot*, like putting on the tallit, entering a Sukkah or reading from the Torah. Rabbi Bunam answered: "It is so no-one should ever think that since the time or place is not appropriate to utter God's name in a blessing, so that they should pause from responding to the needs of another person."[57]

The giving of charity person to person, as it is described in most Jewish sources, is not discriminatory. The beggar does not need to be related to you, nor to be a Jew, nor to have any link with you whatsoever for it to be a *mitzvah* upon you to help him if you can. In our Torah, the *mitzvot* of giving, of attending to straying animals, to lost property and building your house safely are directed at benefitting anybody even though they speak of doing these things for your brother.[58] It is, of course, not literally your brother for whom you should do these things, but for anyone who is in need and whose plight is obvious to you. It was Cain the murderer who denied that he was his brother's keeper.[59]

---

[57] Rabbi Bunam of Pzhysha (1765–1827)
[58] E.g. Deuteronomy 22:1-8
[59] Genesis 4:9

The Jewish scholar Maimonides made a very well-known ranking of *tzedakah*, of the Jewish responsibility to give a share from the bounty we enjoy. The worst way to give, he said, is to give with a glum face and resentment. Towards the top of his ranking of eight ways of giving he put giving in a way in which the giver gives anonymously and does not insist on knowing the identity of the recipient. At the very top of the ranking Maimonides put "helping the needy with a gift or loan or partnership or by enabling them to find employment so that they may become independent."[60]

Maimonides was writing from a Jewish standpoint but this is a principle shared with people of many religions and none. It is often illustrated by the principle of "Give a poor man a fishing rod rather than a fish". Incidentally, Judaism would not completely agree with that if it meant that you denied him the fish when he was starving.

How do we fulfil this *mitzvah* in our day? In Britain Tzedek is a Jewish charity which works with the poorest people in the world. As a small charity they don't work on the scale of Oxfam or Save the Children. Rather, they encourage Jews to become involved with individual projects. One of these a few years ago involved an impoverished Himalayan village in Nepal. The depth of the poverty of this village came from the fact that the villagers had nothing to sell outside the village, thus they could do little more than subsist from day to day and were at the mercy of the weather and had no resources to fall back on if their meagre crops failed. There was one thing that they had in abundance and that was milk from their yaks. In the villages and towns at lower altitudes their milk would have been popular, but by the time they got it there it would be sour.

Tzedek raised just £3000 to install an intermediate technology refrigeration system in the village, based on utilitising mountain ice and snow. The result is that the village now has a substantial cash income

---

[60] Mishneh Torah, Hilchot Matanot Aniyim 10:7-14

from selling its milk and is in a much safer position if troubles should ever come.

That is a charity at work, but what can an individual do? In tandem with the growing sophistication of world finance, micro-finance has become more sophisticated and diverse. This is the system by which the poorest people of the world can get help to get tiny enterprises, like the refrigeration plant in the Himalayas, off the ground.

It is now possible for anyone who wants to fulfil the *mitzvah* of "helping the needy with a gift or loan or partnership or by enabling them to find employment so that they may become independent" to do so from the comfort of their own computer screen. For example, there is a bank called Oikocredit, which was founded in the 1970s by the World Council of Churches. This bank has over 200 million Euros out in loans to tiny enterprises in the poorest parts of the world.

Any individual who would like to invest in these kinds of enterprises can do so by putting a small amount of money in an account with this bank, by which you then own a share in the loans. You even get a small dividend every year. You will know that your money is enabling a farmer in Ecuador to buy a coffee mill, a women's self-help group in Ghana to trade in clothes, a woman in India to scrape a living by selling pencils and stationery in her village and more like that. The bank has branches in many countries around the world, including the UK.

There is currently no Jewish micro-finance fund available in which individuals can invest. The American Jewish Funds for Justice enables institutions to invest in micro-finance by making loans to fledgling enterprises in the most destitute US communities. The American Union for Reform Judaism, through its Chai Investment programme, advocates that all synagogues should dedicate a percentage of their assets to such loans, making a very cogent case which you can download from the website of the Religious Action Centre. But in Britain so far, nothing.

The *mitzvot* of Judaism build from the ancient into the modern day. The Torah scroll is beautiful and old and made with generations old technology. But Judaism is a religion of past, present and future. We need to seek out new ways to do the duties of a Jew, in our worship, in our learning and in our doing of good deeds for others. To do ancient things like reading from the Torah, contemporary things like learning in your Sunday religion school and to do new things like finding ways truly to help the poorest people half a globe away. Micro-finance is an excellent tool with which Jews should join all peoples of good will and care.

# The Beginning Of A New Era

THE WORLD IS not about to end. However, just suppose it was and each of the seven billion people on the Earth were told to leave this planet and take with them their fair share of the Earth. It is really quite staggering just how much of the Earth each of us would be entitled to. If the Earth were divided up evenly between the seven billion inhabitants of this planet each of us would get about one trillion tons to take with us.[61]

You would have thought then that, if so much of the Earth is available to each of us, humanity cannot really have had that much impact upon the planet. Indeed humans have only existed on Earth for less than 1% of 1% of its history. In one rather fun image of the shortness of human history in Earth terms, if you unrolled a typical roll of toilet paper, which is around 400 sheets long, to represent the history of the Earth, the entire time of the existence of the human race would be in the final millimetre of the final sheet of the roll, and recorded human history in the last one tenth of a millimetre.

We have been here for such a little time and we are still tiny compared to the total mass of the planet but we have certainly made an impact. Right now 90% of all of the world's plant activity is found in ecosystems under human control. Our ability to have a fighting chance of feeding seven billion people, six billion more than inhabited the world in the first years of Reform Judaism two centuries ago, is due to our ability to speed up the fixing of nitrogen for fertilisation. Our collection of domestic and farm animals together with ourselves greatly outweighs the number of every other type of large animal on the Earth. One single mine, the Syncrude mine in Alberta, Canada, will in its lifetime require the moving of thirty billion tonnes of earth. Though this is actually rather less than

---

[61] *The Economist*, 28 May 2011, pp13 and 83-85 – the source of most of the statistics in this piece.

each of our personal allocations of the planet, it is still equivalent to two years' worth of the sediment flow of all of the rivers in the world put together, a flow which is 20% less than it was fifty years ago because of the fifty thousand large dams which have been built over that half century. There are now more trees on farms worldwide than there are in natural forests.

The human impact on the world is so great nowadays that many geologists suggest that Earth has left the Holocene era that began ten thousand years ago. The Holocene era was characterised by relative stability in temperature on Earth, which created the conditions for humanity to spread out over the Earth and to thrive. They say that we have now entered a new geological era, the Anthropocene. Now Holocene just means "entirely recent" era, but Anthropocene, a word coined by Dutch Nobel Prize winner Paul Crutzen, means the era where human activity determines the behaviour and situation of the planet. He dates the beginning of this era to the invention of the steam engine in the late eighteenth century.

Human activity here means the way that we farm, the scale on which we change the balance of chemicals in the air. Human activity means the way that we allocate resources between us so that the poorest people need to denude forests, which fix nitrogen in the soil and swallow carbon dioxide in order to live. Human activity means that the rich live without regard to their huge use of resources. Human activity means the environmental costs of the meat we eat.

To suggest that it is now human activity that determines the future of our planet is in a way to reverse the trend in science which took humanity out of the centre of things, when Copernicus found that the Earth revolved around the sun and not the other way round, when James Hutton proved that the Earth's fossil record showed that our planet was billions and not thousands of years old, and when Charles Darwin showed humanity to be just one twig on one branch of the evolutionary tree of life.

55

The Anthropocene theory means that Torah, especially the Book of Deuteronomy, ends up being just what our tradition says that it is – the blueprint for the world. In our Torah and especially in *Devarim*, Deuteronomy, we are told that the way that we behave will determine the rains that we need for our agriculture, in the passage which has become the second paragraph of the Shema, "This will happen if you listen carefully to My commands which I give you today, to love and to serve the Eternal your God with all your heart and all your soul. I shall then give your land rain at the right time, the autumn rain and the spring rain, so that each one of you can harvest your own grain, wine and oil. I shall also give grass in your fields for your cattle, and you will eat and be satisfied."[62] We are told that our care for the poor and dispossessed, the orphan, the widow and the stranger will determine how long we will be able to live on our God-given land.[63] We are told that the Earth is ours conditionally, in covenant with the teachings that God gives us. We do not own the Earth, although we may impact it hugely.

Torah seems to prepare us for the responsibility required by our entering the Anthropocene era, the era when our essential security as a species on our own planet seems to be determined as much by our own actions as by the uncontrollable actions of tectonic plates and natural processes. It only truly prepares us, though, if you see Torah, as Progressive Judaism does, as a continual unfolding of revelation which inspires us to act in the world of today with the ideas and knowledge of today.

Torah begins with one person, then two, Adam and Eve, and shows them learning responsibility as they are tested with the Tree of Knowledge.[64] It then expands our contact with our spiritual history to one family, Abraham and Sarah's. We follow them in the Book of Genesis every year as they learn to be in Covenant with God and take on mutual obligations in order that their family can have the success to grow. When we enter Exodus and right up to the Torah portions that we read in Deuteronomy

---

[62] Deuteronomy 11:13f
[63] E.g. Deuteronomy 16:20
[64] Genesis 2:9ff

we become a people, responsible for each other, with obligations to protect each other's safety, security and dedication to God and especially to protect the Promised Land. Deuteronomy sets us up in relationship to each other as Jews, wherever we may be, with the sense of a spiritual centre in the Land of Israel, with the sense of care each of us for one another, especially if we are not well favoured in the world, in need of a loan yet needing to be treated with dignity, if we are orphans or without family.

It was beyond the time that the written Torah occupies that Judaism developed the tools to extend its message in order to give us a hold in the era in which we live. Jeremiah's reaction to the exile precipitated by the destruction of the Temple was to say, "Pray for the peace of the city to which you have been exiled for in its peace you will have peace."[65] That is, be concerned and active in making the world around you liveable, wherever you are. We built our Rabbinic texts on the foundation that we should love the stranger as we love ourselves and that we should help the poor of the wider communities in which we live, whether Jewish or not, because, in this behaviour are "the ways of peace".[66]

Now that we live in a society so hugely expanded even from the days when our Reform Judaism first began, in a world with seven times the population of that at the beginning of the nineteenth century, our Judaism must surely be concerned with the human effect on that world. We should be good citizens of the Anthropocene era, helping to ameliorate the effects of mankind on the planet. We cannot shrink back into thinking that all that matters is our own people and we cannot shrink away from acting as if God has given us stewardship of the world. He has, and its effects, both good and challenging and even potentially evil, are all around us.

There are seven billion of us because we have learned how to steward the world enabling it to feed us all. A good, though not large enough,

---

[65] Jeremiah 29:7
[66] Babylonian Talmud Gittin 61a

proportion of us live comfortable lives. We are, though, greatly challenged by the effects on the climate and even on geological behaviour that our human activity now creates. The Jewish response, a response for all humanity actually, is to understand ourselves as being in covenant with the world. It will support us if we care for it, just as God is with us if we are loyal to Him.

This is a remarkable era and I doubt if any of us would wish to go back to the peasant, subsistence existence that was the maximum expectation of so many before our days. But the days of taking the Earth for granted are over.

# Jewish Trade Should Be Fair Trade

RABBIS IN BRITAIN often find it helpful to learn from American congregations, where resources on a different scale to those that we are used to enable experimentation and ambition that we can adapt to our congregations. I have spent some time, for example, at Temple Rodef Shalom in Falls Church Virginia. It is a Reform congregation about the same size as ours and enjoying the same diverse programme of activities that we enjoy at my synagogue. I was there to learn from some of the great ideas for Jewish engagement put into action by the congregation and to meet with their Rabbi Amy Schwartzman.

Approaching the synagogue, I was met by two graphic illustrations of the values of this innovative congregation. One was a huge Israeli flag attached prominently to the front of the building, and a second flag proudly saying that Rodef Shalom supports Israel. And by the way there was no security at the synagogue – no need for it apparently! The second was an open shipping container full of furniture, toys, clothes and other donations destined for Washington's poorest residents, left by members towards the synagogue's Mitzvah Day.

The synagogue is located under an hour's journey from the Pentagon and Washington DC and many of its congregants are active on the Washington political and civil service scene.

Rabbi Amy Schwartzman gained a national name for herself in the US, back in September 2003, when she was one of sixteen rabbis invited to meet with President George W. Bush. It was a rather unusual meeting because normally US presidents meet with lay leaders and not clergy in the Jewish community. Rabbi Schwartzman was the only woman rabbi among the group, which included male rabbis mostly from the Orthodox movements and a disproportionately small number of Conservative and Reform rabbis as well as US Forces chaplains. She told me then that whilst to President Bush everybody was Rabbi Shapiro or Rabbi Gluckstein, he insisted on calling her Amy. Folksy, but pointed one suspects.

The reason why Rabbi Schwartzman's presence was noted by many newspapers was not because she was a woman rabbi or a Reform rabbi. A very healthy proportion of the non-orthodox rabbis in America are women. Rather it was because of what she said at the meeting. The issues that all of the other rabbis brought before President Bush were around Israel, the case of Jonathan Pollard, the man held on charges of spying for Israel, and the president's faith-based initiatives as they relate to the Jewish community. Rabbi Amy, when asked by George Bush about what concerns she brought to the meeting, replied: "Since you came into office, the number of people in poverty has increased by three million. My religious faith, as well as yours, compels us to reach out to people on the fringes of society, the poor in particular, and we clearly need to be more responsive to this segment of our nation." She continued with a pointed criticism of the president's welfare bill for not including sufficient child care for single mothers in search of work or job training. "You are creating a situation where a huge number of poor who are single parents have no vehicle for child care. Half the states have waiting lists for federally funded child care programs."

This caused something of a furore in some quarters of the Jewish press where (and feminists will note the language here) Rabbi Amy Schwartzman was accused of haranguing the president. Amy herself reported that the trouble with the meeting was that the rabbis and the president spoke as if the only issues of interest to the Jewish community were Israel and Jews themselves. Rabbi Schwartzman told a reporter that she was, "surprised and disappointed that the group did not represent the ideological spectrum of the American Jewish community. . . . I felt I was surrounded by people who were simply patting the President on the back." As one of Amy's Reform colleagues reported, it seemed that other matters, such as poverty and health care, are viewed as secular concerns, beyond the legitimate scope of a dialogue with rabbis.

But our Torah makes absolutely clear that care for the poor and underprivileged is a core Jewish issue, central to the whole concept of *kedushah*, holiness. In Leviticus Chapter 19 we are given many examples of what Jewish holiness means, from the setting aside of a corner of your field for the poor and the stranger to glean, to not deferring to the rich and powerful in justice, to caring for the dignity of the elderly, to the use of fair weights and measures, to the care and respect due to the blind and the deaf. It is crystal clear that Jews cannot only be interested in Jews and say that they are practicing religious Judaism. Our Jewish ritual, our Jewish peoplehood, our Jewish theology, all, to my mind, must be bound together with the desire and the action of trying to make the world a better, fairer place if we are to fulfil the true meaning of our *mitzvot.*

Most of us will be aware that the choices that we make as consumers each time we fill our shopping baskets make a great difference to the well-being of the people of the world. The man or woman who has picked our mange-tout, grown the beans for our coffee, sewn our shoes, uprooted his staple crops to raise flowers for our table in South America or Africa or Asia is today our poor neighbour whom we should love as ourselves, because once we know that we can make a difference, we should do so.[67]

In the Midrash Leviticus Rabbah, Rabbi Yonah comments on the verse in the Psalms which reads, "Happy is a person who considers the poor."[68] He notes that it is not written, "Happy is a person who gives to the poor." We should consider well how to work with the poor of the world whilst preserving their dignity.[69]

We who are ostensibly the beneficiaries of it need to be aware that free trade between nations in the world today, which brings the produce of the world to our tables, is neither free nor fair. Rabbi Janet Burden in Liberal Judaism's *Just Action* leaflet quotes John Hilary from Trade Justice saying that the so-called free trade system could best be likened

[67] Leviticus 19:17
[68] Psalm 41:2
[69] Midrash Leviticus Rabbah 24:1

to throwing an average person into a boxing ring with a heavyweight boxing champion. Ostensibly the fight would be fair (one-on-one) but there would be no doubt as to the outcome.

The traditional Jewish system of price regulation called *ona'ah* would not allow those with extra financial muscle to exploit others. A transaction was void if the price charged was less than a sixth below or above the independently established market price. This was in response to the verse in Leviticus: "If you buy or sell anything to one another, you shall not wrong one another."[70] This did not stop prices moving to the benefit of consumer, but it meant that there was a balance in trade which ensured that no one could usurp a market instantly or push prices down so far that they made people destitute.

That is what happened in the coffee market before the Fair Trade Movement began, and it still is the case for coffee farmers who do not benefit from it. The contrast could not be greater. The price that is paid to farmers in Africa and South America when they sell to fair trade purchasers is a minimum of $1.41 per lb. The global market price has fallen as low as 45 cents per pound in recent years. There are many other examples where the situation for farmers who are producing for fair trade purchasers differs greatly from the situation for farmers who are not.

Judaism sees reasonable competition in trade to be a good thing. In a dispute between the rabbis in the second-century Mishnah as to whether a trader could compete on price, promotion and product benefits, the majority of rabbis said that fair competition was a praiseworthy business practice which works to everyone's benefit, the issue being whether a trader could give away nuts and snacks to children who bought at his market stall.[71] But if we are to be people who "consider the poor" should we not go further and use our muscle as consumers to relieve poverty by buying wherever possible products which we know have been fairly traded?

---

[70] Leviticus 25:14
[71] Mishnah Bava Metzia 4:12

If a child came to your house and offered to wash your car for 25 pence, which would take him let's say an hour, surely you would insist that at least you paid him or her a couple of pounds to do so, yet the farmers who in the developing world are not working on fair trade terms do just this: they grow your bananas for wages of much less than 25 pence an hour.

Responding to an initiative by our youth club, our synagogue now uses fairly traded tea and coffee in our kitchen, but how deeply are these issues acted upon beyond hot drinks?

Amos the prophet asks: "Are we not like the Ethiopians?"[72] The question is rhetorical. A human is a human is a human. We are like the Ethiopians, and if a little effort from us can enable another person to live a life of more dignity and happiness, then the Jewish code of holiness commands us to care for our needy brother in Ethiopia or anywhere else by not taking unfair advantage of their weak economic position. Fair trade is surely holy trade.

---

[72] Amos 9:7

# Jewish Memory
# and Texts

# It's Not For The Survivors To Remember

WHEN YOU ARE the oldest child in your family, as I am, you don't get to spend much time as the singer of *Mah Nishtanah* at the Seder. This duty was mine for only a couple of years before it was passed down the family to my younger siblings. But I did get a consolation prize. That was the duty of opening the front door of the house to Elijah. Now Elijah may not have shown up but having something to do at the Seder in the bit after dinner when not very much happens was certainly a bonus.

Most families have a tale of something which happened one year when they opened that door. My mother-in-law remembers when opening the door to Elijah they discovered a policeman on the front doorstep. Tantalisingly she cannot remember what the policeman was doing there or what happened next. A family in our community once opened the door to their cat, who was promptly renamed Elijah in commemoration of the event.

Why Elijah? What is he needed for? It seems that the two customs – that of opening the door at this point in the Seder service, traditionally right after the *Birkat HaMazon* (Grace after Meals) and the drinking of the third cup of wine and during the saying of *shfoch chamatchah* (pour out Your wrath), and that of pouring a fifth cup of wine for Elijah, developed separately. The fifth cup practice was in wide use by the twelfth century and the door opening practice certainly by the sixteenth century. This makes them actually rather modern practices, while the basic Seder that we enjoy had developed almost in its entirety more than a thousand years earlier.[73]

Rabbi John Rayner explains the Ashkenazic practice of opening the door as having been a precaution against those who put about the blood libel

---

[73] Mishnah Pesachim Chapter 10

against Jews, accusing us of using human blood to make matzah. With a door opened at the Seder we were opening our practices to inspection by all. Rabbi Naftali Silberberg gives an alternative explanation, that by opening the door at a time of gathering our family together we are expressing our trust in God's protection. Our Exodus puts God's redemption at the centre of the story: note that Moses is not mentioned once in the Haggadah. In the Haggadah our release from slavery was God's work. No need for Elijah then. Just for memory and trust.

Except that the point at which the door is opened is also the traditional point for pouring the cup for Elijah. Why? The third cup has been drunk and it is therefore time to prepare the fourth and final cup of the Seder, or is it? There are five promises made by God quoted in the Haggadah from the same passage in the Book of Exodus: "I will lead you out from under the Egyptian yoke; I will deliver you from their bondage; I will redeem you with an outstretched arm; I will take you as my people."[74] Each of these promises merits a cup of wine at the Seder.[75] But in the same passage there is a fifth promise, "I will bring you into the land which I solemnly promised to give to Abraham, Isaac and Jacob." Surely this promise too should merit a fifth cup of wine?

It seems that in some Jewish traditions it did, but the tradition remained uncertain. Step in Elijah the prophet, of whom we hear on the Shabbat before Pesach, Shabbat HaGadol, in the Haftarah from Malachi.[76] The final verses of that Haftarah portion promise the return of Elijah the prophet before the end of days to help us to "Remember the Torah of Moses ... with all the statutes and judgments." So therefore, reasoned the rabbis, he will help us to resolve all of the outstanding questions of Jewish practice so that we know what to do, including whether or not to pour and drink a fifth cup of wine at the Seder. Indeed, since Elijah arriving will, in our mythology, herald the coming of the Messianic Age, we will indeed be about to be brought into the Promised Land again in fulfilment

---

[74] Exodus 6:6-8
[75] Babylonian Talmud Pesachim 99b
[76] Malachi 3:23-24

of that promise. By the twelfth century the fifth cup had become Elijah's cup filled but never drunk, until Elijah comes!

We are now used to the idea that the fifth promise of redemption, that God would bring us into the Land, is not celebrated at the Seder except by the hopeful action of filling a cup for Elijah, which has now been joined together with the ritual of opening the door. There is a strong reason why this is so, based on the essential motif of the Seder.

There was a choice made by our ancestors when the Haggadah was first compiled two thousand years ago, when they put together the story which in the words of the Mishnah "begins with degradation and ends with glory".[77] It need not have stopped with the redemption from Egypt, and then the sudden jump in the song *Dayenu* to being in the Land and building the Temple. The Haggadah could have told the story of coming into the Land. It could have included the Joshua narrative of the struggles to inherit the Land and the settling of the tribes. That would have made the fifth cup of wine and its accompanying promise make sense. Something deliberate is happening in keeping us on the journey itself, not feeling that we have reached the Promised Land, the destination.

It is because of the essential task of the Seder, to ensure that each one of us feels that we have personally made that journey from enslavement to liberation, but yet do not know how far we will get. The world is not yet redeemed, even if we are able again to go to, and politically control, the land of our people, Israel. It too is not yet perfection. The journey continues and we travel on that journey, begun for us as a people by the Exodus from Egypt and not yet concluded.

The Haggadah is not there to tell us our history. If it were, then the Joshua narrative would have to be part of it – rather it is there to build our memory from generation to generation. As Rabbi Jonathan Sacks puts it, "History answers the question, 'What happened?' Memory

---

[77] Mishnah Pesachim 10:4

answers the question, 'Who am I?'"[78] That is why the Seder takes place at home as a family, in the heart of the creators of your identity, the most powerful location for telling us who we are and a location which is utterly portable, needing nothing more grand than a place to sit, some symbolic foods and a book to pass on the memory that once we were slaves and now we are free to serve God.

No priest is needed at the Seder, no representative of Moses is needed, no rabbi is needed, no surviving ex-slave who actually walked out of Egypt is needed, and even the prophet Elijah need not be standing at the front door for us to feel the joy of the journey towards redemption. Memory and identity are passed on intact from generation to generation to generation through this most participative ceremony of the Seder.

The weeks after Pesach in the Jewish calendar since 1948 have been full of reminders that we are still on the journey, hoping that one day we will truly have received an answer to the promise that we will be brought into the Land. Just days after we leave the seventh day of Pesach and the annual recharge of our memory and identity is completed, we have to remember the tragic attempt to kill off our entire people not even a generation ago, when Yom HaShoah is commemorated twelve days after Pesach began. It was a deliberate choice of the Knesset in 1951 to place Yom HaShoah on this day so close to Pesach, commemorating as it does the Warsaw Ghetto uprising, when we fought back against Nazi oppression. Then eight days later we commemorate Yom HaAtzmaut, Israel Independence Day, still only a step on the journey, but Israel is as close as we have been to seeing God's fifth promise fulfilled for two thousand years.

Both Yom HaShoah and Yom HaAztmaut, and Yom HaZikaron which precedes it, are there for all Jews to participate in, just as Pesach is. Yet it does not tend to work that way. Both Yom HaShoah and Yom HaZikaron

---

[78] Jonathan Sacks, *The Home We Build Together* (London: Continuum, 2007), p116

have been regarded by many Jews as days for the survivors and their families only. Whilst on Pesach it is a customary jump for a Jew to say, "This is what God did for me when I came out of Egypt", we have not yet got to the point where we commemorate Yom HaShoah and Yom HaZikaron by saying, "This is what I remember, for this is my identity and my memory."

We must ensure that the memory of the Shoah is held by the community as a whole, not depending on the survivors and their second generation. We transcend slavery and oppression by remembering ourselves to have been redeemed from slavery, so too we transcend the evil of the Nazis by remembering ourselves as survivors whether or not we were personally their intended victims (a crazy concept because, of course, we were their intended victims, as the Wanasee conference in January 1942 enumerated the Jewish populations of every country with a substantial Jewish population with the aim of obliterating it). We transcend the threat of war under which Israelis live by remembering those who have been killed as if we might have been that person. Judaism in the twenty-first century demands of us that we continue the Pesach skill of memory for two more weeks each year, for we live in momentous times.

Elijah is not here yet – the questions of whether and how this world could be better are not answered yet, we have not yet completed the journey as a people. Together we carry our memory so effectively on Seder night. We should continue to carry the memory of those who suffered even more recently so that they can live on through us, their fellow Jews.

69

# Mind Your Language

THIRTY THOUSAND PEOPLE were on the march. Encouraging them on was a band of harps, cymbals, drums, tambourines and rattles. King David was at the front, leading his people towards Jerusalem in triumph. In the middle of the procession was the Ark of the Covenant, symbol of God's power among the people, containing the tablets of the Ten Commandments and the broken fragments of the original tablets which Moses had smashed in anger at the incident of the Golden Calf.

The procession reached the top of a hill, a threshing floor in a windy, exposed place. The oxen pulling the cart, on which the Ark was transported, stumbled. The Ark swayed and looked like, horror of horrors, it might even fall off the cart. Uzzah the Levite put his hand forwards and steadied the Ark. Right then and there he collapsed and died! What happened?[79]

Every year when we read the Sedra Chukkat, the Torah portion in the Book of Numbers, where Moses, having led the Children of Israel for the best part of forty years, is sacked from his post by God, told that he will not enter the Promised Land, there is a loud harrumph of disapproval from one of our synagogue's regular Shabbat worshippers. This man, who has followed the unfolding story of the Torah every Shabbat during the year, is disgusted that the simple action of hitting a rock to obtain water should deprive Moses of his position and be, in his opinion, so harshly punished. His loud disapproval is a wonderful example of instant Torah commentary.[80]

I would imagine that if he heard the story from the Second Book of Samuel of Uzzah dying after he tried to help by steadying the potentially falling Ark he would be similarly shocked and upset.

---

[79] 2 Samuel Chapter 6
[80] Numbers Chapter 20

The Rabbis, of course, wondered just what Uzzah might have done that death resulted from the apparently meritorious act of steadying a falling Ark of the Covenant. In Midrash they provide a few possible explanations.[81] One is that he was meant to be concentrating when employed in such a holy task and his inattention to his duty as a Levite is what so angered God. Another is that the Book of Numbers states that the Ark of the Covenant is meant to have been carried on the shoulders of the Levites, so what was it doing on an ox cart?[82] Perhaps this act of laziness was Uzzah's idea, and so his punishment was just.

Another, based on the particular choice of Hebrew verb for the averted falling of the Ark, was that Uzzah was in such a panic as the oxen stumbled that he relieved himself! My favourite interpretation is that Uzzah let out such a stream of swear words as the Ark swayed that he could no longer be entrusted with its care in such a large and impressionable company of Israelites. And the final one, which is not in our classical collections of Midrashim, is that Uzzah died suddenly, as people do on rare occasions, and then David and the Israelites connected his death with what he had done to steady the Ark as it risked falling.

I managed to end up in a thumb splint for two weeks following an injury. My story was disconcertingly similar to that of the hapless Uzzah the Levite. Alan, our synagogue's caretaker, and I were picking up the moveable Ark which we use for family services and parallel Shabbat services so that we could move it between locations in the synagogue. Where the handles are placed is very low and the Ark began to topple forwards as I picked it up. I foolishly steadied it with my thumb, causing a tendon injury. Ow! However, the worst imprecation I let out was "Oh flip!" So I guess I am safe from Uzzah's fate.

If Uzzah's punishment (if punishment it was) seems unfair at face value, then so does Moses's for hitting the rock, and Adam's and Eve's who are

---

[81] Found in Babylonian Talmud Sotah 35a and Bemidbar Rabbah 4:20
[82] Numbers 7:9

ejected from the Garden of Eden.[83] At face value the Torah contains many examples of seeming injustice.

How then can the Torah be for us the inspirer of right behaviour? How can it be our guide? Do we have to read selectively perhaps, listening only to those parts of the Torah where the face value meaning seems to us to inspire justice?

It is easy to read the Ten Commandments and be proud of the wisdom contained within. It is easy to read the Holiness Code in Leviticus and hear that we should love our neighbour as ourselves and that we should leave the corners of our fields for the poor and hungry and be inspired by its vision of social justice.[84] But throughout this year, as every year, there are tough passages to hear. In our lectionary, which guides the readings we hear from our Torah, there are passages which we do not get to hear in our synagogue because they are too tough to take at face value, such as the rape of Dinah,[85] the curses for failing to observe the covenant in Deuteronomy,[86] the outer reaches of the purity laws in Tazria – Metzora.[87]

There is something in Reform Jewish history that makes it difficult for us to deal with the challenging passages of the Torah, both those which we hear in the synagogue when we read and those which we still omit from our three-yearly cycle of readings. Early Reform Judaism saw one of its missions as being to restore the primacy of the Bible in Judaism, as opposed to the centuries of Rabbinic interpretation recorded in the Mishnah, Talmud and Rabbinic commentaries and the Midrashim. That was because this Rabbinic interpretation had got Judaism stuck, so that it could no longer bring our religious wisdom to the modern world. Systems of authority had meant that Jews tended to accept one single line

---

[83] Genesis 3:23
[84] Leviticus Chapter 19
[85] Genesis Chapter 34
[86] Deuteronomy 28:15ff
[87] Leviticus Chapters 12-15

of Rabbinic authority as being true, rather than interpreting the Bible as man's striving after God's will, for themselves.

Early Reform Jewish services and synagogues gave prime place to liturgy which was from the Bible itself and ensured that Bible readings were translated, that our religion schools taught the Bible raw without requiring a particular line of interpretation. We did not study our Torah through Rashi's eyes, Rashi being a particularly authoritative biblical commentator from the eleventh century.[88] Rather we studied our bible with all the tools at our disposal: biblical archaeology, historical, sociological and anthropological knowledge. You can still see this trend represented in a very healthy way in the inclusion of the Nelson Glueck Museums of Biblical Archaeology in the Reform Jewish Hebrew Union College Campuses in Jerusalem and the USA.

However, this early Reform Jewish approach for us today poses a spiritual challenge, perhaps even a spiritual danger. Early Reform Judaism tended to ask what the truth of the Torah and Bible as a whole was in the day in which it was written. What was the organisation of society at the time of the Torah that meant the orphan and the widow were in a particularly bad situation? Did the Red Sea really part, what were the volcanic or wind conditions that could cause it to do so? Was there really a mass Exodus from Egypt or did a confederation of Canaanite tribes create a founding myth to unite them in the worship of the One God? These questions remain important and Reform Judaism will never shy away from the search for historical and anthropological truth.

But archaeology and anthropology cannot inspire us to action in the service of God and of our community. Our task as we hear the Torah is to study it for truths and values leading to action. Our traditional interpretations in the Midrashim, the Rabbinic works and even in the Psalms are a great aid to this because they give us the starting point of

---

[88] Rabbi Shlomo Ben Yitzchak (1040-1105), French commentator on Judaism's classical texts.

other's strivings after spiritual truth.[89] But we must also be brave and interpret Torah using our own spiritual resources.

For example, when we hear about Adam and Eve leaving the Garden of Eden it is fully valid to see this as a metaphor for the growing up, independence and responsibility which we must all share to live a full life. When Moses is sacked as leader we can question what it takes to move on from a position of leadership and to bring on and empower a new generation. When Uzzah dies as he steadies the Ark we can question how we ensure the sanctity and grandeur of our holy spaces and ritual objects which point towards the service of God.

These are my personal interpretations for today, and in the spirit of living Reform Judaism they are put there to be argued with. Our synagogue and all Reform synagogues should be centres where the Torah, the Bible, and our traditional literature are studied, made accessible, argued over, dissected and put back together to build us spiritually as Jews. Hearing the Torah in our Shabbat services is only the beginning.

---

[89] E.g. Psalms 78,105,106,135, which retell Torah narratives in an interpretative fashion.

# Telling Stories Of The Past For A Better Future

WHAT IS UNIQUE about being human? It's not the ability to walk or hunt or form family groups, most mammals can do that. It's not the ability to nurture our young. Birds care for fledglings with tender care It's not the ability to be ingenious. Watch a squirrel finding its way into a bird feeder. It's not even the ability to use tools. If a chimpanzee finds a tasty nest full of termites he will use a stick to get them out and will use a stone to crack a nut. What is unique about humans, says Professor Mark Pagel, is the way in which we use language to implant thoughts directly into each other's minds, giving rise to social learning.[90]

Chimpanzees will never transform the stick that they use to get into the termite's nest into a shovel, nor will they swop banging a nut on a rock for walking into a shop and buying nuts which are ready shelled. They are not able to pass on to each other what they have learned about how to do things better and more effectively.

Our fossil record shows that the ancestors of humanity made pretty much exactly the same kind of hand axe for a million years, 40,000 generations. Then 200,000 years ago our language skills evolved and developed enough that we could begin social learning from each other. This meant that I can do what you can do without putting in the time and effort to develop it for myself.

I can see how you flake the flint from your hand axe and become as good a hunter as you. Something, though, in our God-given faculties meant that we did not keep this ability to learn just to the smallest family groups, guarding it jealously. Rather, we used it to develop co-operative society and shared and exchanged. Since then this has meant that humans have been able to spread worldwide using our social learning

---

[90] Professor and head of the Evolutionary Biology Group at the University of Reading.

skills to adapt to our environment, while other species are stuck wherever their genes best suit them. Witness the more than two hundred countries represented at the Olympic Games from the frozen north to the baking south, all able to perform to peak physical ability.

Critical to the social learning which has enabled humanity at its best to steward the world as well as live with its vagaries is the telling of stories. We don't build our groups simply by giving instructions. We use the most effective way to pass on values, ideas and emotions so that each of us learns to build our understanding of the world ourselves. We tell stories.

We ground our children's understanding of Judaism by telling them tales of their spiritual ancestors. Few would argue with the proposition that a good part of our synagogue's early-years Jewish education, our religion school, and the home Jewish education which we encourage should be the telling of Bible stories. No-one would propose that instead of telling our children about Abraham, Miriam, Esther and Moses we should be discussing the current state of Jewish philosophy.

We followed this principle and included some well-told Bible tales into our daughters' bedtime story routine when they were young. Though we have done so with little self-analysis, clearly behind our telling of these stories was our wish to begin to build their Jewish identity and acquisition of Jewish values by means of telling them tales that they will come to see as their own.

I was discussing our telling of Bible tales with a friend of mine, who would describe himself as a liberal humanist. We wondered together what tales he could tell to his daughter to fulfil the same role as a Jew or Christian's Bible tales, a Muslim's tales of the Prophet, a Hindu's tales of the pantheon. He suggested that he too could search history to tell the tales of exemplary people. He suggested Martin Luther King, Mahatma Ghandi, William Wilberforce, Nelson Mandela and the like. The only trouble for the liberal humanist is that all of these were or are essentially religious men, King the pastor, Ghandi the Hindu ascetic, Wilberforce, late of the Hendon parish and endower of many of our local churches, even Nelson Mandela was brought up in the Methodist church. Thus at least one aspect of their lives would fail the humanist test.

Judaism has always been deeply conscious of the power of story narrative to build identity and to grant authenticity to our message. The Book of Deuteronomy, in which Moses reprises the laws and commandments which are set to govern the Children of Israel and establish their covenant with God, does not begin by listing the laws in order of their importance or any other such dull device. Rather it begins with the relating of the tales of the wandering, of the forty years since Mount Sinai, with the history of the people he is addressing. In this way Moses cements the identity of the people whom he will be guiding and establishes the authority of the claim of such laws upon them.

So great can be the power of the telling of historical tales in establishing and maintaining identity that almost all Jews, even those who are close to secularism in their Judaism, use the device yearly at the Seder service. Indeed Rabbi David Saperstein, past Director of the Union for Reform Judaism's Religious Action Centre, reports on the time when he was among a group of Jews who were consulted by the Dalai Lama a few years ago. The leader of Tibetan Buddhism, living in exile, was searching for the secret of our people's longevity when our connection to our religion's land of origin had been broken. The Dalai Lama said that he could see in the Seder service the whole secret. It has been the continually repeated tale of our history impressed deeply on each generation that has sustained us in our Diaspora. Through our story we have made our rootlessness our triumph.

The power of Jewish history poses a special challenge to Reform Judaism – especially when you call it Progressive Judaism, implying as this does that it is our Jewish mission to move forwards, onwards, upwards, and presumably away from our history. What are we to do with the ability of tale telling to carry our message to our next generation and to cement the identity of the current generation?

Generally speaking, we use it as much as any part of Judaism. Understanding that Bible stories and the Midrash, which enhances them, personalise our religious values and give a personal dimension to the development of our religious tradition ensures that we will continue to tell them to our youngsters. Inevitably we add a Reform Jewish slant in which, for example, the military exploits of Moses are less celebrated than his qualities as a leader, the courage of Esther is more celebrated than the revenge that she takes against the Persians, where Jacob's guile in duping his brother Esau is not glossed over. We will continue to teach our history as a people, aware that our particular interpretation of Judaism and Jewish authority is borne on the wings of Judaism's encounter with modernity. Thus a Reform Jewish approach to Jewish history inevitably takes the surrounding cultures into account, rather than making the specious claim that Judaism has always been isolated from such influences.

Essentially the Reform Jewish task is to be grounded in history and the tales of our people and yet to transcend them. In doing so we follow a tradition stretching back at least to the times of the Mishnah and Talmud, when the Rabbis of the turn of the Common Era and the five centuries thereafter developed a Judaism that recognised the importance of the destroyed Temple and its style of worship to the history of religion, and yet took its rituals into a new generation no longer living exclusively in the land of Israel. So, for example, the Passover sacrifice was turned into the home observance of the Seder, the priests bringing in the Sabbath with sacrifice were replaced by lighting the candles and drinking a cup of wine. The centralising authority of a nation, its priesthood and kings, was replaced by the meritocracy of the rabbinate and the Jewish community.

Our history will continue to ground us, our stories will always have great value. Our task is to use them as starting points for responding to the challenges of our day.

# The Value Of Hebrew

IN 1937 LEO ROSTEN published "The Education of H*Y*M*A*N K*A*P*L*A*N." Many have laughed with Hyman Kaplan as he makes a new language of the English he is supposed to be learning with the hapless teacher Mr Parkhill at the American Night Preparatory School for Adults. What else would a new Jewish immigrant from somewhere unnamed in Russia expect the plural of cat to be but K*A*T*Z? Who else could the US president who freed the slaves be but Abraham Lincohen? If you have not read the book – do, it's hilarious. I have had two opportunities to spend time in ULPAN classes, those total immersion in Hebrew classes which teach enthusiasts and new Israelis together the language of the State of Israel. The classes have been full of characters just as vivid in my memory as Hyman Kaplan, Miss Mitnick and Mr Parkhill.

My Ulpan in Jerusalem, to which Leo Baeck College sent me in 1995, included the wonderful Victor, a new immigrant from Georgia, who just couldn't get a single word of Hebrew, and was looking in vain for a shop in Jerusalem where he could buy pork sausages like he remembered from Tbilisi. Then there was Ruti, the teacher who kept the class going together with her humour. In 2005 my Sabbatical leave included two weeks at Ulpan, not in Jerusalem, but rather in South Hampstead United Synagogue, the annual Ulpan then run by Nitza Spiro and her team of teachers under the name of the Spiro Ark. The classes included their share of characters, most of us taking a couple of weeks from our regular work to propel our Hebrew into another league.

At the Spiro Ark Ulpan there was the shy Japanese student whose interest in Judaism in her native country had led her to Britain to learn Hebrew. There was Hannah, the girl who had just finished her A levels and one week later enrolled for Hebrew classes with people twice, three, and four times her age. There was Malcolm, a retired accountant, who

79

spoke his Hebrew so slowly that you completely lost the thread of what he was saying by the end of each sentence. There was Nitza Spiro herself with her boundless enthusiasm to teach.

But the most memorable person I met at Ulpan that summer was a man of eighty-two who was there because he had decided to make Aliyah to Israel and fulfil a childhood dream. He had left Egypt in 1956 with his wife and two young daughters in the wake of the Suez crisis. Back then, half a century ago, he would really have wanted to make Aliyah but he knew that it would not have suited his wife, they would not have been happy. Instead they settled in the London suburb of Hendon, brought up their two daughters, were blessed with grandchildren and lived a good and decent life. In April that year this man's wife had died and he was facing life alone, with the support of his daughters. However, as he said to me, in a perfectly nice part of London people don't really talk to each other in the shops, people don't walk, you cannot sit outside at a café and while the time away with friends. So at eighty-two, newly widowed, he decided to follow the dream of his youth. He found a place in a retirement community in Netanya and was now, through the Spiro Ark, learning enough Hebrew to get his new life started. All of us over the fortnight of the Ulpan came to admire this man and his resolve.

Meanwhile, what was I doing there? In a way I was doing penance, atoning for the sin of insufficient competence in Hebrew. I remember when my synagogue was visited by a large group of sixteen-year-olds from the Leo Baeck Education Centre in Haifa. Before the service the synagogue chairperson, who had lived for some years in Israel, spoke to the youngsters about Jewish life in North London, and I came in at the end of her talk to welcome the group to the synagogue. I should have been able to do so in Hebrew, but I couldn't. I was tongue-tied by lack of confidence so ended up speaking with them in English. So I resolved that one of my Sabbatical aims would be to get my Hebrew level well up, hence the Ulpan and weekly lessons with Nitza Spiro!

Spoken Hebrew is set to become increasingly relevant in synagogue life in London over the coming years. Estimates suggest that there may be as many as seventy thousand Israelis living in London today. There are thought to be over three-quarters of a million Israelis living outside the State of Israel. Any synagogue in an area with a high proportion of Israelis should surely be ensuring that Israelis feel at home and may make the leap into synagogue participation which is a new experience for many. Being able to converse in their first language, Hebrew, at least with the rabbis, will be important in the coming years.

It may yet be some time before we hear much Hebrew spoken in our synagogues as well as hearing it read or sung in prayer. Undoubtedly, in all forms of Progressive Judaism the use of Hebrew in our services has increased in recent years. I will look at why this might be so below, but first we should remind ourselves that praying in our vernacular, for us in English, is as old as Jewish formal prayer itself.

We conclude our services with the Kaddish, a prayer in Aramaic, not Hebrew, which was the common language of Jews during the Roman period and after. The Mishnah tells us in words from two thousand years ago that the Shema and the Amidah, the core prayers in the service, together with the Grace after Meals, can be recited in any language.[91] A very old tradition in the Talmud makes it explicit that the reason for this is because the very word that begins our key prayer, Shema, means both hear and understand. We cannot truly worship God unless we can understand what our mouths are saying.[92] This view was confirmed by great Jewish authorities throughout the ages.

Judah HeChassid in the twelfth century in Germany asserted that, "Prayer takes place only when the mind understands, and if the mind does not know what proceeds from the lips, what good is that to the worshipper? Therefore it is better that those who do not know Hebrew

---

[91] Mishnah Sotah 7:1
[92] Babylonian Talmud Berachot 13a and Sotah 32b

should pray in a language they understand."[93] Maimonides confirms that all prayers, including the Shema, may be recited in any language. What matters is the intention and care with which they are recited.[94] Joseph Caro, in the Shulchan Aruch, where he codified the state of Jewish law in the sixteenth century, agrees with him.[95]

This may surprise you. Another great authority who confirmed that it was best to pray in a language you understand with *kavannah*, in his *Shulchan Aruch Ha Rav*, published in 1814, was Shneur Zalman of Lyady, the first Lubavitch Rebbe!

So with this line of clear tradition, what happened in 1818, just four years later, to make forty rabbis, including the famous Chatam Sofer, sign a pamphlet stating in words of one syllable that it was forbidden to pray in any language other than Hebrew or to change a word of any traditional prayer? Simple. In the Reform synagogue which opened in that year for the first time in Hamburg, people, men as well as women, prominent educated people, actually started doing it, publicly offering services conducted largely in German. Rabbi John Rayner suggests in his booklet *The Language of Prayer* that with that act Orthodox Judaism was born too. The 1818 opinion is supported by Rabbi Michael Epstein in his *Aruch Ha Shulchan*, the most prominent Jewish legal code for the first years of the twentieth century. He wrote that "nowadays, and for the past eighty years, it is forbidden to recite the Shema or the Tefillah or any of the blessings in any language other than the holy tongue of Hebrew". The general permission to pray in the vernacular which had been the thrust of most Jewish authorities, was, so to speak, rescinded once Reform Judaism was born and praying in the vernacular of worshippers became a reality for congregational prayer.[96]

---

[93] John Rayner, *Jewish Religous Law: A Progressive Perspective* (London: Berghahn Books 1998), p.85
[94] Mishneh Torah Keriat Shema 2:10
[95] Orach Chayyim 62:2; 101:4 and 185:1
[96] Books of Tekhines, prayer in Yiddish, primarily used and compiled by women, had been in existence for private prayer for many years already.

So if we have every good authority apart from the reactionary to empower us to pray in English, why are Reform Jews using an increasing amount of Hebrew?

Of course any answer is multi-factorial. Progressive Judaism in all of its forms has been seeking to build competence in our source texts so that we can soundly base our Judaism, as well as our humanity, in Jewish tradition. For that truly to work you need Hebrew. Many more of us visit Israel than even a generation ago. There we find a Jewish community which virtually outnumbers that of the USA, their language is Hebrew, and so we grow more comfortable with hearing it. We too as Progressive Jews are finding our own Judaism more and more relevant in Israel, so much so that the Israeli published textbook which I used for my Hebrew lessons at ULPAN included examples of *Reformit* or Progressive Jewish practice alongside Orthodox Jewish practice in the example stories it gave. Israeli creative prayer is finding its way into our Reform Jewish prayerbooks. *Seder HaTefillot*, the Reform Siddur published in 2008, included poems written for the siddur of the Israel Movement for Progressive Judaism. In a past generation all of the source material for creative prayer would have been British or American and in English. As we travel more and visit synagogues overseas we find that Hebrew competence means we can participate in services everywhere.

But if this is so then there is much work to do. Many of us find it difficult to understand much of the prayers we are saying with our level of Hebrew. Many others have yet to grasp enough Hebrew to participate. It is never too late to learn Hebrew. Following his experience in the Spiro Ark Ulpan, Eli succeeded in learning Hebrew and continued to live a happy life in Netanya using the language of Israel and Jews throughout the world every day.

# Making History In Eighty Metres

IN ANY JEWISH congregation in Europe there are many people who have lived through and witnessed events which will make history for many generations to come. Each year at our synagogue we hear from members of our community who are the children of Shoah survivors. Their parents lived through some of the worst acts of man to man ever in history, witnessing at first hand the horror of the Nazis, and we, through them and their children, are the inheritors and guardians of this memory.

I am fortunate that this historical burden is not directly imposed upon me as my family were in Britain throughout the Nazi period. But in 2008 my family and I experienced first-hand a little bit of history in a journey of forty seconds and eighty metres. We were staying in Cyprus, in the Greek south, and although there have been car-accessible border checkpoints through which one might travel to the Turkish North for the past few years, that week was the very first since the Turkish invasion in 1974 when it had been possible to walk down the central street of the divided capital Nicosia, Ledra Street, and cross right into Turkish Nicosia.

The street in the centre of Nicosia's medieval quarter was split in 1964 during an outbreak of communal fighting, when British peacekeepers laid barbed wire between the street's Greek and Turkish Cypriot sectors. Since the ceasefire in 1974 there have been two sides of a main road left as a UN-controlled no-man's land, right in the middle of the city, through which no-one can pass. Just before April 1st 2008 the two sides of the island agreed to open, Red-Sea-like, a passage between the buildings. You entered one end of the 230-feet-long walk and, passing by four UN soldiers through a corridor lined with blue-painted hoardings, found your way to the Turkish side where, after some inevitable queuing, you would receive a day visa to enter.

On one side of the street, the Greek side, you feel distinctly in Europe; on the other side, the Turkish side, life is distinctly Middle Eastern, the foods, the drinks, the Turkish script, the bazaar.

Inevitably, both sides of the Cypriot struggle have quite different narratives of what happened to divide the island. On the Greek side the story is all about Turkish aggression and the injustice of Turkish settlers moving into the Northern part of the island. On the Turkish side, in the free newspapers you are given when you cross, the narrative is about Northern Cyprus's rejected attempts to make peace and re-unite with the south.

Pesach is the essential narrative of Judaism. It is how we establish who we are and what it means to be a Jew. It is the festival which sets us out on our journey not of 230 feet but of millennia. Like I know that Ledra Street, April 3rd 2008, in Nicosia, was the start of something special, I know too how my people started.

In 1947, David Ben-Gurion appeared before the United Nations Commission weighing Jewish and Arab claims as the Mandate period was ending. Ben-Gurion's remarks focused on Jewish history, with Pesach at the centre: "Three hundred years ago, a ship called the Mayflower left for the New World ... Is there a single Englishman who knows the exact date and hour of the Mayflower's launch? ... Do they know how many people were in the boat? Their names? What they wore? What they ate?"

He contrasted this record with that of the Jewish people. "More than 3,300 years before the Mayflower set sail, the Jews left Egypt. Any Jewish child, whether in America or Russia, Yemen or Germany, knows that his forefathers left Egypt at dawn on the 15th of Nisan. ... Their belts were tied and their staffs were in their hands. They ate *matzot*, and arrived at the Red Sea after seven days...".

Rabbi Elliott Kleinman asks why we know this. Perhaps the children do not know the detail of the story of the Mayflower in such detail because it is not the journey that's so important but rather the destination, as we learn the history of the United States. For us Jews, though, the story of the journey is all. Our Haggadah tells us about the journey.

It didn't have to be that way. The narrative of the Haggadah could have been the Book of Joshua, the biblical book which tells us what happened when the Children of Israel reached the Promised Land. Wouldn't that make more sense? After all, we say in our current Haggadah that our story starts in degradation and ends in glory. But this is not the way we do Pesach. Reaching the Promised Land is not the Haggadah narrative. Rather we hear about the Exodus from Egypt. Similarly on Sukkot we sit in booths reminiscent of the simple shelters needed on the journey and we have chosen not to use this festival, for instance, to celebrate the Temple which, the Bible tells us, was inaugurated on Sukkot.[97] Again, it's not the destination but the journey that matters.

In his book, *The Home We Build Together*, Rabbi Jonathan Sacks quotes Isaiah Berlin who said that, "All Jews who are at all conscious of their identity as Jews are steeped in history." Rabbi Sacks critiques Isaiah Berlin's insight. He writes that it's not history which Jews are steeped in. History, historia, dates, political systems, clashes of nations, events are not what matter to Jews and Judaism. History is someone else's story – maybe we are back in it with the creation of the State of Israel, but it's not been the Jewish experience to be the makers of history. Rather, he says, what we are steeped in is memory, *zachor*, a word which occurs 169 times in the Bible, notably on Pesach to say *zecher litziat mitzrayim*, the memory of the Exodus from Egypt.[98]

History is someone else's story but memory is my story. That is why we tell the story of Pesach not as history in our Haggadah but rather as memory handed down parent to child, in the words of the Mishnah as if

---

[97] 1 Kings Chapter 8
[98] Jonathan Sacks, *The Home We Build Together* (London: Continuum 2007), pp115-117

we came out of Egypt ourselves.[99] History answers the question "What happened?", like in Cyprus the Ledra Street passage through Nicosia opened again. Memory answers the question, "Who am I?"

My family and I walked through and experienced Europe and the Middle East in a single afternoon. Memory is telling the story as your own, which of course is how the Seder service came about and developed into a home ceremony family by family, which is the most powerful location for identity. The Seder and the memory of Exodus was of course utterly portable, even into the concentration camps, even into Soviet Russia.

Passing on the memory is joining a journey. Rather than as the reaching of a destination, memory enables us to be part of the journey. The journey out of Egypt from slavery to freedom continues to this day and until Elijah comes, until the Messianic Age begins, it will continue with us Jews among the peoples of the world who aim to make the journey ever more bearable through fighting for social justice.

It is much the same with the State of Israel. The bringing about of the State of Israel is not the final destination for the Jewish people. This epoch-making achievement is yet one major step on a journey. Rabbi Eric Yoffie, past president of the Union for Reform Judaism, wrote: "Our connection to Israel is rooted … in a religious vision and in a dream of what Israel can become [the journey upon which it is on] … For Reform Jews the stakes are especially high. If we fail to establish a significant presence on Israeli soil and do not become a powerful force in the next generation, we will have consigned ourselves to the margins of Jewish history."[100]

Israel, too, is a story unfolding. We must be part of that story and able to pass it on.

---

[99] Mishnah Pesachim 10:5
[100] *Reform Judaism*, Spring 2008

There is a custom of Greek Jews, maybe even those in Cyprus, of keeping a bag with them at the Seder, almost packed for the journey. Yemenite Jews have a walking staff by their side and will even get up and walk around the table to demonstrate that they are on the journey itself.

Enjoy the journey. It is your life and the length of your days. And pass on the memory so that your children, grandchildren, and great-grandchildren will walk with you by your side.

# The Not-Messiah Of Golders Green

THE PROPHET ELIJAH is alive and kicking and visiting homes in North West London. At least he is if children in Akiva School, Finchley, year 6 are to be believed. I had the privilege of teaching the year 6 class at the Akiva School. I was asked to teach them why we have a cup of Elijah on the table at Pesach. Who is Elijah – and why does he get to come to our Sederim, or not?

It turns out that Elijah has indeed visited the Sedarim of many of the young people. When the cup of Elijah is filled up at the Seder, mysteriously some of it seems to disappear before the Seder is over. It's as if Elijah has come to drink from it. For one Akiva student Elijah has appeared a couple of times at her Seder with woolly beard and hair and looking rather like one of her uncles. For another, apparently, Elijah metamorphoses into a fly which her Grandpa always seems to be able to spot somewhere in the room after the door has been opened.

Now these Elijahs clearly come from the same place as the tooth fairy. And as we all know the tooth fairy is real! People really want to believe that a better time is about to come. What do you do if you are the one they think is Elijah?

This has happened to poor Raj Patel. Raj Patel is a thirty-seven-year-old economist who grew up in Golders Green, London. He has written popular books about problems in global food production and ideas for solving the inequalities that result. He recently published a book called *The Value of Nothing*, about how we might fix the system which resulted in the 2008 financial collapse.

*The Guardian* newspaper reported that he appeared on an American talk show to plug his book. Soon afterwards followers of the Scottish mystic and theosophist Benjamin Creme started to email and write to him asking him if he was truly Maitreya, the world teacher predicted by Mr Creme. If so then Raj Patel is the embodiment of an eighteen-million-year-old saviour who has been resting in the Himalayas for the past two thousand years. Followers have come half way across the world to meet him and the messages have not stopped. But for poor Raj Patel this is all becoming a bit much. As he says, "People are very ready to abdicate responsibility and have it shovelled on to someone else's shoulders ... whenever there is going to be someone who's just going to fix it for you, it's a very attractive story. It's in every mythological structure." Raj Patel is not taking this very seriously, nor are his parents who have created a t-shirt for him based on the line in Monty Python's *Life of Brian*, "He's not the Messiah, he's a very naughty boy."[101] But do we take it seriously when we invite Elijah into our homes, and how does he inspire us to take our own responsibility for the future?

The prophet Elijah first appears in the First Book of Kings at a time of crisis among the people of Israel.[102] At this time the Northern Jewish kingdom under King Ahab and his wife Jezebel had turned to idolatry, setting up temples to the fertility god of the Canaanites, Ba'al. In the process Jezebel had massacred hundreds of prophets, men and women with an acute spirituality who were the religious rather than cultic leaders of their day. In disgust at the situation, Elijah went to meditate in the wilderness, where, in a fashion that was to happen many times in his life, God saw to his feeding, via a helpful raven. Returning from the wilderness, he revived the son of one the supporters of God's prophets from apparent death.

During a drought and resultant famine he was found by Ahab and ordered to Mount Carmel to challenge the prophets of Ba'al to see who could bring rain by succeeding in getting their god to set fire to a sacrifice. Elijah won the contest, having soaked his sacrifice with scarce water.

---

[101] *The Guardian*, 20 March 2010, p11
[102] 1 Kings Chapter 17

Back in the wilderness, to which he escaped from a livid Jezebel, Elijah is again fed by a miracle and has a vision of God, neither in the fire nor earthquake which happen around him but rather in a still small voice – a *bat kol*. He finds his successor Elisha, whose story occupies the Book of Kings after his, and who is also a miracle worker and tormentor of corrupt kings.

Elijah's most notable ultimatum to a king occurs when Ahab steals the vineyard of the neighbour to his palace, Naboth, killing him in the greedy process. Elijah speaks truth to power and Ahab dies wretched. Elijah continues as a critic of the corruption both of Israel and Judah and, when the time comes for him to die, he simply does not do so, rather ascending in a chariot of fire as he casts his mantle down onto his successor Elisha.[103] He appears one more time in the Tanach – at the end of the Book of Malachi, which we read on Shabbat HaGadol just before Pesach, as the Prophet who will return at the end of days to turn the hearts of the parents to the children and the children to the parents, later interpreted as being able to solve all insoluble problems.[104]

What an amazing character, one of the most sharply drawn of all the biblical personalities! Dramatic, fearless, driven and passionate, a fighter for justice with right on his side, with no patience for the processes of history to work their course slowly, and with a good measure of the ability for miracles to happen around him.

Elijah's cup and Elijah's legendary presence at our Sedarim do not appear in the Talmud, which tells us the state of the Pesach ritual in the sixth century CE. He first enters Jewish ritual five hundred years later – about a thousand years ago – during a time when we could really have done with him back.

Elijah's role in the Talmud is as the solver of problems which seem otherwise insoluble, and also the announcer of the coming of the Messiah

---

[103] 2 Kings Chapter 2 (the end of the Elijah narrative)
[104] Malachi 3:23-24

or Messianic Age. He never died in the Tanach, so surely he could come back! His chair is present at every Brit Milah, circumcision, because he complains that the Israelites are not following the covenant, thus he is there from the eighth century or so onwards to supervise the entry of every Jewish boy into the Brit, the covenant with God.

In the eleventh century, under the shadow of the Crusades, he was clearly needed again. It is at this time that the song Eliyahu HaNavi enters the Havdalah ritual, asking that Elijah the prophet send us news of better times ahead, preferably at the end of Shabbat, which the Talmud says is the right time for his arrival.[105] He also enters the Birkat HaMazon, the Grace after Meals, at around this time – *HaRachaman Hu yishlach lanu et Eliyahu HaNavi.* If God is our comforter, *HaRachaman,* let Him send Elijah now!

His appearance at the Seder has two roots. One is that in some Jewish rituals there was a fifth cup of wine – not just four – corresponding to the fifth promise of Exodus Chapter 6: not only **I will bring you out** from under the burdens of the Egyptians, and **I will deliver you from their slavery**, and **I will redeem you** with a outstretched arm, and with great judgments; And **I will take you to me for a people**, but also **I will bring you in** to the land. How should we know whether to drink this fifth cup? Let Elijah come and solve the problem.

It is the second root that keeps him there. It is the words *L'shanah HaBa'ah B'Yerushalayim* which end the Seder. Next year in Jerusalem, next year in a world redeemed. Not a thousand years, nor a hundred years, nor ten years but next year. Elijah is the symbol of Jewish radical impatience. We do not have forever to improve the world. The slaves should be free now, the poor should not be hungry from tomorrow, the prisoners of conscience should be released today, the risks of climate change should be addressed immediately and hatred between peoples should cease this year.

---

[105] Babylonian Talumud Eiruvin 43b

Elijah never said, "Let's wait till Ahab and Jezebel pass away and then deal with the problems of the time." Elijah did not say, "Ahab is powerful, he can take what he wants." Elijah's courage and passion said do it right away, right the wrongs. Each year his character, his example, should inspire us so that when we sit down to our next Seder we can know that we have done what we can to bring us all at least one step closer to Jerusalem.

As well as his cup brimming full of sweet wine, the symbol of Elijah is the open door, opened by a child at the Seder, hope opening the door to hope. Elijah tells us that we must open the door to our future. It is why our synagogues must never be closed to the community around us. Rather, our doors must be as open as possible to a better future.

We cannot assume that Elijah will be here to help us to work out the solutions to our problems, we cannot place our responsibility on the shoulders of others, as the not-Messiah of Golders Green, Raj Patel, said. So in the meantime we must be the Jews with radical impatience for a better future. If not Jerusalem next year, then at least a better North West London!

# Jewish Ritual

# The Meaning Of Kashrut For Today

IN HIS BOOK *Chasing Shadows*, where Rabbi Hugo Gryn recounted his childhood in Berecovo, he wrote about the life of the synagogue in the town. We are used to hearing a sermon weekly, a *drasha* every Shabbat to bring our Torah portion to life in our day, given by a rabbi or guest preacher. In Berecovo, in keeping with *minhag* in sub-Carpathian Ruthenia, the rabbi would preach only four times a year and the synagogue would be full to bursting to hear his carefully considered words of guidance and, hopefully, wisdom. One of those four yearly occasions was *Shabbat HaGadol*, the Shabbat immediately before Pesach.

Why was this Shabbat the one for a grand sermon? Because in Berecovo observance of the *mitzvot* was the foundation of the learning that the rabbi would teach and the complication of observing Pesach kashrut was worthy every year of a grand sermon so that the community would not err. This was combined with a good dose of hope for the future based on the hope for Elijah the prophet to herald the Messiah. After all, the traditional greeting for Pesach is "Have a happy and kosher Pesach."[106]

Now fast forward to 1995 and it is Pesach in London. I was leading a week-long trip to Israel for fourteen- and fifteen-year-old Reform and Liberal Jews from a number of synagogues. It was the third day of Pesach and we were waiting in Heathrow airport for our departure. The young people were given half an hour free to do as they wished. What about half of the group of twenty-five wished to do was to buy a sandwich. It was clear that many of them were not keeping kosher for Pesach in any way. I was shocked.

In Israel of course things were much easier as there was no choice but to keep kosher. Even McDonalds in Jerusalem, as my young companions discovered to their delight, transferred to potato flour rolls for Pesach.

---

[106] Hugo Gryn, *Chasing Shadows* (London: Viking, 2000)

They all spent the week kosher for Pesach and I think gained much from the experience, and the joy when on day five of the week bread returned to our diet was a sight to behold.

Kashrut is bound up with Judaism in several ways. Its essence is that we choose to forgo certain foods at certain times, even though they may be good for us, tasty and easily available. Some of the foods which are not kosher most of us would consider disgusting, like worms, guinea pigs as eaten in South America and, the first non-kosher food listed in Torah, the limbs of live animals.[107] But most non-kosher foods are just fine to eat.

Maimonides writes in his *Guide to the Perplexed* that pork meat is delicious, it's just not kosher, though he also writes that, due to all of the pigs running around, the villages of the Franks are very dirty!

What is the role of keeping kosher in Judaism? In Leviticus 11, where we hear about the non-kosher animals, fish and birds, it is simply said that its purpose is to bring a Jew who observes it closer to God, *kadosh*, to holiness.[108] So keeping kosher enables us to bring Godliness into every mouthful that we eat. Even if we do not pray three times a day we eat three times a day or even more often.

It's not about health. In the Middle Ages, Jewish systematisers who were asking the "why" questions that had not previously been asked in Jewish literature began to suggest that kashrut was God's gift to Jewish health promotion. Perhaps in contrast to other peoples around, Jewish communities were suffering from fewer health problems and they became convinced that kashrut was the root cause. The trouble with this analysis is that if you consider kashrut to be somehow God-given then, if health promotion was the reason, it was not a job well done. The fattiest foods can be kosher, potentially poisonous mushrooms are

---

[107] Derived from Genesis 9:4
[108] Leviticus 11:45

kosher, you can get food poisoning just as easily from poorly stored and prepared chicken as from pork or shellfish.

But kashrut is about one more general aspect of healthy eating which has repercussions in a broad scope of life. That is, training for self-discipline and control. If you cannot eat anything you fancy whenever you fancy it then you have the foundation for not giving into other harmful aspects of life. Hence the use of the word kosher for a decently conducted business deal. Remember the root meaning of the Hebrew word *kasher* is fit or proper, proper to eat, proper to do.

Woven into kashrut is simply respect for life. We are not to eat blood because it is the life force of an animal or bird. Thus if you buy eggs from a kosher food shop they will be white-shelled rather than the brown-shelled eggs now general to all supermarkets, the better to be able to hold them up to the light in order to inspect them for forbidden internal blood spots before use. The separation of milk and meat rule is interpreted as being needed to separate life-giving milk from death-caused meat, beyond the insult of boiling a kid in its mother's milk.[109] Shechitah has at its root a method of slaughter intended to cause an animal as little distress as possible at the time of its inevitable death. The current threat to shechitah, which is the proposal that all meat killed by its method should be labelled as "not pre-stunned", is effective only to the extent that people don't believe shechitah to be the kindest method.

A fourth basis for kashrut is based on the root meaning of *kadosh*, holy. It is that kashrut enables us to approach holiness. The *shoresh,* root, of *kadosh* means "separate". But what does kashrut separate us from? Something impure, that brings something undesirable into the world, like lack of self-control, lack of respect for life, like forgetting God in daily life. But of course for many Jews kashrut has become the factor that separates them from non-Jews or even their own Jewish friends and

---

[109] Exodus 23:19

family because the degree that they choose to take it to separates them from enjoying regular social interaction with them.

Behind Passover kashrut are all of these and also a sense of history in the very substances which sustain us. To me this has always meant that even if you choose not to observe many of the other aspects of kashrut you cannot properly participate in Pesach and its meaning without observing a reasonably high degree of Passover kashrut. How better to feel that you yourself came out of Egypt than to eat the bread of affliction, matzah, for seven days? How better to remember the value of freedom in our history than to clear out the substances that puff up like the pride of our erstwhile captors? How better to ensure that the memory of Pesach past in yours and the Jewish family is preserved than to have the taste of your own *charoset*, Passover cakes and biscuits passed down from generation to generation?

All of this was different a century ago in Reform Judaism. The Pittsburgh Platform in which American Reform rabbis set out the principles of our Judaism in 1885 states: "We hold that all such Mosaic and rabbinical laws as regulate diet, priestly purity, and dress, originated in ages and under the influence of ideas altogether foreign to our present mental and spiritual state. They fail to impress the modern Jew with a spirit of priestly holiness; their observance in our days is apt rather to obstruct than to further modern spiritual elevation." Kashrut was out, for the time being. Thus a nonagenarian member of our synagogue told me that he remembered being given ham sandwiches after choir practice at West London Synagogue in the 1930s in the sure knowledge that none of the members would object.

Reform Judaism, like all authentic Judaism, grows, learns and develops. Now the 1999 Pittsburgh Platform, when a group of American Reform rabbis gathered in the same town to restate Reform Judaism, puts things differently. "We are committed to the ongoing study of the whole array of *mitzvot* and to the fulfilment of those that address us as individuals and as a community. Some of these *mitzvot*, sacred obligations, have long been observed by Reform Jews; others, both ancient and modern, demand renewed attention as the result of the unique context of our own times."

And so it is with British Reform Judaism: kashrut is back. But it is broader. Reform Judaism is no longer willing to wipe large areas of Jewish practice off the agenda. When it did, it did so because, as far as we were concerned, the duties of the heart, or rather of the intellect, always trumped the duties of the limbs or body. Reform Judaism is progressive. We live in, react to and sometimes try to lead the real world in response to God and humanity.

Kashrut is a matter of degree, and it starts from the principle that there are some foods which it is not right to eat, even though they are edible, because it is not fitting for a person who lives by Jewish values to consume or to encourage their production.

Rabbi Zalman Schachter-Shalomi writes, "In every age Jews exist to ask the question, 'What is Kosher?' Kashrut is a continual effort to find what is clean pure and good for the natural processes of the universe."[110] A Reform Jew today joins every Jew in finding their own degree of kashrut. As Reform Jews we add to the structures which have been built by Jewish tradition our knowledge that the ways in which animals are raised and slaughtered can range from those with no respect for the animal's well-being, only its productivity, to those which recognise we should use every means possible to avoid *tza'ar ba'lei chayyim* – causing a fellow living being pain. Many Progressive Jews will therefore consider buying free-range and not battery eggs and insist on meat from free-range animals being an aspect of kashrut today. Some choose to be vegetarian or vegan. Many will include conditions of the workers who produce our food to be part of kashrut by seeking out fair trade in production. Many will feel that we need to include the *mitzvah* to steward the world in a

---

[110] Zalman Schachter-Shalomi, *First Steps to a New Jewish Spirit* (Woodstock: Jewish Lights 2003), p49

way which does not wreck the environment or its productivity for future generations in our understanding of kashrut, and thus seek out sustainably fished cod, or foods which have not been air-freighted.

In Torah itself the only reason given for the laws of kashrut is that they help us to approach God's holiness and purity.[111] This means that kashrut cannot only be something static, based on the approval of a particular rabbinic authority which charges a licence fee to place a seal on a foodstuff. Instead, it is one of the dynamic ways in which we interact with creation in order to try to bring the world a little closer to God. It is a wonderful aspect of Judaism that we can do this through every mouthful that we eat to fuel our bodies.

---

[111] Leviticus 11:45

# No Cathedrals In Judaism Please

IN MY EARLY twenties, in 1984, I was on a backpacking holiday in Israel with three friends. One Shabbat evening we were in Jerusalem. Two of us were Jewish, two were not. The other Jewish fellow and I thought that it would be an interesting experience to take advantage of the informal system whereby any Jew can go to the Western Wall (known in Hebrew as the Kotel) on a Shabbat evening and will be found hospitality for the evening with a Chassidic family in Mea Shearim.

After our dinner in Mea Shearim, my friend and I were given beds for the night in a yeshiva a few hundred yards up the hill from the Kotel. At about one o'clock in the morning I was unable to sleep, so I got up, took my copy of the Progressive Siddur, and walked out into the fresh Jerusalem air towards the Kotel. A couple of minutes later I found myself one of only three people at the wall, the stars above me and complete silence surrounding me. I began to pray and felt a profound sense of inner peace. After an hour or so I walked back to the yeshiva and returned to bed genuinely spiritually refreshed.

In summer 1994 I was also in Israel for some time. As I was staying in Jerusalem, I took the opportunity to visit the Kotel one weekday afternoon. As I crossed the plaza to approach the wall I was assailed by a Jewish man in black garb who asked me for some *tzedakah*, charity, to help him to support his family. I gave him a few shekels and proceeded to the wall. I was immediately approached by another, frankly prosperous looking, Chassid asking for charity. I told him that I had already given to another man and that I now wanted to pray at the wall. Perhaps I should have been more generous, but he would not leave me alone, even when I was trying to pray at the Kotel. Eventually by rather rudely ignoring him I was able to stop him from persisting with his *schnorring*. That summer's visit to the Kotel provided the opposite of spiritual refreshment for me.

Back in 2012 a Progressive Jewish woman, Anat Hoffman, was arrested for praying at the Kotel because she was wearing a tallit and refused to desist from doing so. The controlling Orthodox authorities at the Wall can really disappoint a Jew who wants a place to pray.

During my time as a student at Leo Baeck College I took many services at the Liberal and Progressive Jewish Communities in Lincoln, Norwich and Peterborough. Each of these cities is dominated by a glorious medieval cathedral. I have been to visit each of them and even participated in an inter-faith service in Peterborough Cathedral. I am often impressed by the air of quiet devotion that permeates these cathedrals even when they are filled with many tourists. And you would never be persistently *schnorred* by a chorister in a cathedral.

What do we Jews have to compare with the Christian cathedrals? Where are our public places for quiet devotion? If you cannot be sure of quiet at the Kotel, where can the Jew go for spiritual refreshment? Where are our Jewish sacred places?

The first sacred site for Jews was the cave which the patriarch Abraham purchased in which to bury his wife Sarah. This was the cave of Machpelah in Kiryat Arba, also known as Hebron.[112] According to midrash, Adam and Eve, Abraham and Sarah, Isaac and Rebecca and Jacob and Leah were buried there, and the midrash tells us that Kiryat Arbah (the town of four) was named for these four pairs. The cave of Machpelah is still in existence, occupied by several sarcophagi of unknown origin.[113]

In the early centuries of the Common Era the cave was covered by a Byzantine church which was replaced by a mosque around the ninth century. Tragically this mosque, with its legendary cave containing the remains of our Patriarchs and Matriarchs, was the site of Baruch Goldstein's obscene massacre of twenty-nine Moslem worshippers in February 1994.

---

[112] Genesis Chapter 23
[113] Midrash Bereshit Rabbah 58:4

Now that the site has been so desecrated, surely the cave of Machpelah can no longer be a place of spiritual refreshment? Truly we Jews have no cathedrals made of bricks and mortar. What could have been our sacred sites are not respected as such in a way that has real meaning for the Progressive Jew. They have been desecrated by avarice, discrimination and even violence.

No place can, of itself, be holy in our Judaism. In our Judaism our cathedrals can, however, be built in time.

Abraham Joshua Heschel, an American rabbi who died in 1972, speaks of the Jewish architecture of time.[114] Our architecture, he says, is built of the Shabbat, the yearly cycle of the festivals, the lunar months, the Sabbatical year every seven years, when traditionally the land was given rest, and the Jubilee every fifty years, when traditionally all property returned to its original owners.

Every Shabbat, as we make our Kiddush, we sing aloud that we and God together have made a portion of time holy. It is important to remember that the extended Kiddush that we sing on Shabbat Evening is not for the wine. We already covered that with the blessing which ends *borei p'ri ha-gaphen*. Our Kiddush is specifically directed at expressing the holiness of the Shabbat itself. It ends with the *chatimah* or closing line, "*Baruch Attah Adonai m'kaddeish HaShabbat*, We praise you Eternal One who makes the Shabbat holy."

But if it is time that is holy for Jews, then what is special about the synagogue, that makes it a worthwhile building? It is the time that we spend within them and what we do together in our services and activities that makes synagogues special. It is the fact that we mark our special Shabbat times and our special festival times in a synagogue that lends a little holiness to their rooms and to their buildings.

---

[114] Abraham Joshua Heschel, *The Sabbath* (New York: Farrar, Straus and Giroux, 1951)

Down the centuries Jews could take their holy times, their Shabbat, their cycle of festivals, with them wherever they went. In the worst times for our people, when synagogues were burnt down and our books were destroyed, we still had our holy times to support and refresh us. In our best times, when we live as well-accepted members of mixed communities, we can create our holy times in rented rooms and school halls just as effectively as in the grandest buildings. Indeed most synagogues have their origins in Shabbat gatherings in members' homes and club houses. The synagogue is important in that it gives a focus and venue to the activities of a congregation, but it is the time that we spend within it that gives it its religious significance.

In our creation story, which we find in the first chapter of Genesis, we can find the first reference to the special character of time in Judaism. In all of the first six days things were created. Things which can be destroyed or misused – the animals, the seas, the plants and humankind. But on the seventh day, the Shabbat, a special time of rest was created. According to the biblical account it was only this aspect of creation that God blessed and made holy.[115]

Indeed the heights of technology can create or simulate all of the other six aspects of creation. We can cross-breed plants, we can genetically engineer animals and we can simulate human intelligence. But science can never create even a nano-second of time. Science can never, of itself, create a moment of time experienced by a human as special. The builders of past millennia could make the beauty of the Kotel, the Western Wall, which was a supporting wall of the Temple, but they could neither stop a *schnorrer* nor an aggressive policeman from spoiling the experience of being there, nor create the spiritual refreshment that I had experienced there once in the early hours of the morning.

No-one can ever possess time. It can only be shared or given. A community can own a grand synagogue but it is only through sharing time within the

---

[115] Genesis 2:3

building that the synagogue becomes the spiritual home of a community. You can feel wonderful in the filthiest of places or awful in the most beautiful. It is only through your experience of the time, of being there, that the place has any power. As Heschel wrote, "Monuments of stone are destined to disappear from the moment that they are built; days of spirit never pass away."[116]

The Jewish perception of God and what God wants us to do is locked in with our concept of time. Heschel wrote, "God has no geographical address nor a permanent residence." That is an obvious point. Yet as children I'm sure that many of us had a conception of God being somehow in the Heavens which then developed to a sense of God all around us. Rather, wrote Heschel, "God is in events, in acts, in time, in history rather than in things. And when God appears to be in things, God may be profaned and driven out, or kept out by the power of our deeds."

Each week that you dedicate your time to be part of the Shabbat you are helping to create a certain holiness in your life. Every occasion that you devote your time to doing something Jewish, helping others, studying, coming along to activities at the synagogue, you are helping to create a certain holiness in your life. Judaism needs each one of us to build its temporal cathedrals.

---

[116] Abraham Joshua Heschel, *The Sabbath*, op.cit., p98

# It Would Not Really Have Been Enough

MANY FAMILIES WHO enjoy their Pesach Sedarim have particular traditions which make them special and add to their quality. Some become so popular that they get incorporated into the Seder meal for a whole section of the Jewish people. For example, the tradition of eating a hard-boiled egg in salt water is a particular Russian and Polish tradition which has no Jewish legal backup, but take away from my father his role in the Seder preparation of boiling up quails' eggs and he would complain bitterly (this being a particular Goldsmith family tradition in recognition of an episode in the Exodus).[117]

Some traditions come to represent something which then becomes shared by many Jews, for example the tradition of adding an orange to the Seder plate done by many people in recognition of the famous rabbi who said that a woman belonged in the pulpit as a rabbi about as much as an orange belongs on a Seder plate. Add an orange to your Seder and celebrate seven decades of women rabbis![118]

And that is even though this is not actually how the tradition started. Susannah Heschel, daughter of Abraham Joshua Herschel and Professor of Jewish studies at Dartmouth College, originally introduced it onto her family's Seder plate. She offered each member of her family a segment, asked them to say the blessing over fruit over their segment and then to eat it in recognition of Jewish lesbians and gays and others who are marginalized within the Jewish community. In this way they could recognise the fruitfulness of all Jews when everyone is able to be a contributing and active member of Jewish life. Spitting out the pips, Professor Heschel says, represents our need to repudiate the homophobia and other prejudices that stop full inclusion from happening.

---

[117] Exodus Chapter 16 and Numbers Chapter 11
[118] The first was Rabbi Regina Jonas who gained Semichah in 1935.

There was a custom that an Indian Jewish family at Woodford Progressive Synagogue used to share. Instead of risking staining the tablecloth with wine poured out for each plague they would put the drops of wine into an earthenware jar and then bury the jar in the garden so that the misfortune of the plagues would not remain in their house. In more grand days back in Calcutta each person in the family would have had a servant standing behind them with their own personal earthenware jar!

Some years ago I joined cousins in Los Angeles for their Seder. There our daughters became the inheritors of our American family tradition. Our daughters were each given a $2 bill for finding the *Afikomen*. These $2 bills are pretty rare, you have to order them especially from the Federal reserve. I remember my delight in receiving my $2 bill back in the 1970s when I was a boy and we were living there.

Some Sephardi Jews at a Seder use a leek or onion to beat each other gently from the moment in the traditional *Dayenu* song when they sing, "Had you supplied our needs in the desert for forty years but not fed us manna from Heaven." Every time the refrain *day dayenu* is sung you get hit by an onion. I'll explain why later.

When I was young, and I suspect it is the same for every young Jewish child to this day, *Dayenu* was the number one song of the Seder. There are none of the nerves of being the child who is singing *Mah Nishtanah*, none of the Aramaic of *Chad Gadya*. Everyone can join in *day dayeinu*, "It would have been enough." It was the loudest song at all our cheder Seders, on the last day of our religion school term.

There is more than one version of *Dayenu*. The Orthodox *Dayenu* breaks down the events of the Exodus and then thanks God for each of them in turn. "Had God taken us out of Egypt but not executed judgement against the Egyptians *dayenu*. If God had killed their first born but not given us their possessions *dayenu*, given us their possessions but not parted the sea *dayenu*, it would have been enough." The Orthodox *Dayenu* takes us from Egyptian slavery to our being given the Temple in the Promised Land. The Liberal *Dayenu*, which I grew up singing, starts with our exodus from Egypt and then goes much further. It moves step by step through Jewish history from Sinai, to the Promised Land, to the Diaspora and then the regaining of Israel until it reaches our day and our continuing responsibility to repair the world.

Whichever way you sing your *Dayenu*, the song is based on what seems to be a ridiculous notion. Has it occurred to you when singing *Dayenu* that of course it would not have been enough? If our foundation story saw us being taken out of Egypt but the Red Sea had not been parted, of course it wouldn't have been enough. Our ancestors would have been swamped by the Egyptian army at the shore of the sea and either killed then and there in revenge for the death of the first-born or returned to slavery. In the Liberal version, of course, it wouldn't have been enough for us to be given the Torah and then for God not to have sent us the Prophets. Where would our Jewish understanding of the care for the oppressed come from? How would our mission to better the world have developed?

Of course, to bring us to today we needed all of the things to which we say *Dayenu* to have happened, and to have happened in the correct sequence. There would have been no point sending us manna until we were in the wilderness. There would have been no point asking us to try to be a light unto the nations until we had prophetic guidance to tell us what that means.

The point of *Dayenu*, of course, is to express gratitude for every facet of our story as a people. There is, in the words of the Hartman Haggadah, "a sense that the Exodus unfolded in many steps each constituting a miracle in itself. The poet feels the living power of each gesture of divine favour, irrespective of the total result ...The principle of *Dayenu*, of giving thanks for, of appreciating even the partial and incomplete, is crucial for living in this uncertain world in which few dreams ever come to total fruition."[119] It is crucial to the happiness of our relationships, where our partners or our children or our parents have little chance of meeting all of our expectations or wishes for them. But we can be thankful for each step that they take in the direction towards us. If we are only appreciative when everything is perfect then we create in our households, our workplaces or our synagogues a sour, critical and unconstructive atmosphere. *Dayenu* says: appreciate each step towards something better.

We could thank God every day for the miracle of being alive and say *dayenu*, that was enough. In learning gratitude to God we also learn to show gratitude to parents, teachers, loved ones and friends, even when their efforts fall short of completeness.

That is why the Sephardi Jews hit each other with leeks whenever they sing *Dayenu*. It is linked with the Torah story of the Israelites who, far from saying "thank you for the manna, this is enough", complained, and in the Book of Numbers recalled with longing the onions in Egypt: "We remember the fish that we used to eat in Egypt, the cucumbers, the melons, the leeks, the onions and the garlic. Now our gullets are shrivelled. There is nothing at all. Nothing but this manna to look at."[120]

If we can take the message of *Dayenu* forwards with us into the year after our Sedarim, perhaps we can learn to be thankful for everything that moves us on a little towards happiness, for every effort that someone makes on our behalf, for gestures of care. Besides, if the Israelites had got all their onions, leeks, garlic and fish, just think what their breath would have smelt like!

---

[119] Noam Zion and David Dishon, *A Different Night – A Family Participation Haggadah* (Jerusalem: Shalom Hartman, 1997), p107
[120] Numbers 11:5-6

# Thank God As Well As The Caterer

IF YOU ARE a group of accountants getting together late night at a conference the kind of thing that you are likely to talk about is some of your nightmare audits, companies that you went into that were hopelessly disorganised, bags of un-sorted receipts going back five years, etc. If you are a group of teachers relaxing after a long training day then it will be nightmare children for whose pranks you perhaps have a grudging admiration. If you are a group of doctors then it will be patients who have given you grief or, if you are social workers, impossible clients.

What then do rabbis chat about when it comes time for the professional small talk? Well inevitably one topic that comes up is simchas, the weddings and barmitzvahs that you are invited to as either a fringe benefit or occupational hazard of the rabbinate. Tales of excess are swapped, of inappropriate entertainment, of drunken uncles, ribald best man's speeches, of collapsing wedding cakes and never, of course, about one's current congregation. So neither is my nightmare simcha story from the congregation which I currently serve.

Most of the time as a rabbi you are invited to the simcha because the family has got to know you either over the years or in the run-up to the life-cycle event which the simcha celebrates; you have become a friend of the family. But sometimes you feel that you are essentially an aspect of the table decorations. There are wonderful balloon arrangements, flowers for the great aunts to take home, a bottle of red and a bottle of white and, on the far left or right of the top table, next to *bubba*, a decorative rabbi, preferably bearded and with dutiful wife to his right, but if Reform and with working spouse then clean shaven and alone will do. The simcha story which I have been known to share when one of these "but you'll never believe the one I went to" sessions starts up took place at the wedding at which I felt most like a table decoration.

The groom was Italian though had been living in England for some years, the bride was English from an originally Italian family. The bridegroom's family, over from Italy, spoke very little or no English. I had cheerfully mugged up on a welcome speech for the chuppah itself in Italian - *benvenuti a nostra ceremonia* etc. Then it came time for the simcha, which took place in a swish London hotel.

I am not quite sure what the family were thinking when they sorted out the seating plan, but certainly the idea that it might be nice for me to be able to speak to someone during the meal had not really occurred to them. Hence on one of those formal top tables there I was on the far left, seated next to the groom's grandmother, who not only did not speak any English, she didn't speak Italian, but rather only Tuscan dialect. Next to her was the groom's father, he spoke only Italian, then the groom's mother, who spoke only Italian. I was separated by four people from the next person to whom I could speak. So I spent that particular wedding smiling at the grandmother and staring into space.

As often, one of my roles at the wedding was to lead *Birkat HaMazon*, Grace after Meals, so at the earliest opportunity I duly led the grace, made my apologies and made my way home.

In the end the only redeeming feature of that simcha was the opportunity to do the *mitzvah* of leading *Birkat HaMazon*. Though my silent simcha was a particular challenge, the simchas I find the most difficult actually are those where I am invited in my capacity as rabbi and am challenged by the request that either we do not do the Grace after Meals, or that I somehow make it shorter than the six minutes or so that it normally lasts.

Sometimes this is done from apparently noble motives, such as that many of the people at the simcha will not be Jewish and thus it is assumed would be bored and alienated by *Birkat HaMazon*. My response to this suggestion is to say that it is then the duty of the person leading the thanksgiving after meals to make it understood what we are doing, to ensure that all of the guests are provided with a translation and transliteration of the prayers and songs and to lead some of the prayers in English so that all can participate. Too often, though, I reckon that the real reason why a few people would prefer not to have *Birkat HaMazon* at their simcha is because they simply do not feel the need to give thanks for what they have eaten and the plenty that they have shared with their guests at their function, especially when they weigh that act of thanksgiving against the benefits of six more minutes of uninterrupted conversation.

The words which give rise to and are indeed included in our *Birkat HaMazon*, "*v'achalta v'sava'ta uveirachta et Adonai Elohecha al ha-arets ha-tova asher natan lach* (when you have eaten and been satisfied then give thanks in blessings to your Eternal God for all the good land which he has given you)," are in the Torah.[121] If asked by someone what the purposes of religion are I would say that this is one of them, to ensure that we do not take for granted the blessings of our lives, however little they may be, but especially when they are manifold.

Religion helps you to create a space and find a structure to be thankful, to God, to providence, to nature, for the goodness that sustains our lives. Having been in the habit of giving thanks, of not taking our blessings for granted, we will then be in a more ready state to respond to the needs of others, because we realise the value of what we have. In our days, when we are asked to respond to the basic needs for food of asylum seekers and refugees in our local area, when we know that the chaos in many countries means that many are hungry in what should be prosperous nations, when some parts of the world suffer from drought or conflict, making basic food needs unmeetable, how can we begrudge six minutes of thankfulness at our family simchas? The final words of the Liberal and Reform *Birkat HaMazon*, words which, incidentally, were written by Rabbi Hugo Gryn, say, "May we not turn aside from the needs of others, open our eyes and our hearts and our hands so that we may share your gifts and help to remove hunger and want from the world."

---

[121] Deuteronomy 8:10

The chance to give thanks, and the context in which to do so, is one of the purposes of religion. Our worship service is full of thanksgiving. Each of the blessings which end each of our prayers is a form of thanksgiving for the aspects of our life that we might otherwise take for granted. We begin our service with thanksgiving for our songs, then thank God for the light of day and for calling us as a people to serve Him. We thank God for our redemption from slavery, for his relationship with our ancestors and for giving us life, for the Sabbath, for accepting our worship, for God's goodness and for the measure of peace that we enjoy.

Each of these pieces of formalised thanksgiving takes the form of blessings beginning *Baruch Atah Adonai*. By their formalisation they can perhaps pass unrecognised, but if we can we should pause and contemplate just what we are expressing gratitude for. Rabbi Meir used to say each of us should find the time and space to say one hundred blessings each day that we are alive.[122] In the traditional three-service structure of the Jewish day there are indeed one hundred opportunities to say *Baruch Atah Adonai*.

On Shabbat, though, the services are reduced by omitting the intermediate benedictions, the sequence of short prayers that we have in a weekday service and thus of course in a weekday evening service encountered at a shivah, which is where many Jews who are not used to praying daily encounter them. So how do you get up to your quota of one hundred "thank yous"? Rabbi Hiyya had a solution for this. He used to keep some spices and sweets on his person and smell them and eat one every once in a while so that he would have to say another blessing of thanks.[123]

A formal structure of thanksgiving, services and Grace after Meals is a great aid to ensuring that we are grateful for the blessings that surround us, for food, clothes and shelter, so that we learn not to take for granted and recognise and want to help with other people's lack of the daily

---

[122] Babylonian Talmud Menachot 43b
[123] Babylonian Talmud Menachot 43b

essentials. As a father I seem to spend large parts of the day reminding my two daughters to say "please" and "thank you" for the things that they ask for and enjoy. So indeed it says in our Torah that God brings us up as a father does a child.[124] Don't let Him down by begrudging the opportunity to say "thank you" for the world we live in, especially when we enjoy so disproportionately many of its blessings.

---

[124] Deuteronomy 8:5

# The Not Mitzvah

MOST SHABBATOT A Bar or Bat Mitzvah celebration takes place in our synagogue. The young person reads from Torah, having been called up by their Hebrew name, shares a D'var Torah giving his or her new and fresh perspective on the Torah portion and participates in the Shabbat morning service. A few years ago a Bar Mitzvah took place in New York of a young man called Rocco. He did not read from the Torah, nor did he give a D'var Torah and neither did he participate in a Shabbat morning service, but a Torah scroll was completed in his honour. If all of that sounds a bit odd for a Shabbat morning you shouldn't be too surprised to hear that the Bar Mitzvah took place not in a synagogue but at the Kabbalah Centre in New York, that Rocco is not actually Jewish and that his parents are the pop star Madonna and the film director Guy Ritchie.

It wasn't really a Bar Mitzvah but it was an important creative rite of passage for his family. Rabbi Jeffery Salkin notes that, among the non-Orthodox, the vast majority of traditional Jewish observances seem to have shrunk. It seems that the substance of Passover Sedarim has shrunk. He senses that fewer people observe *yahrzeit* than ever before. Yom Kippur fasts are shorter.

And yet, even as other observances shrink, Bar and Bat Mitzvah have grown, explosively. What was once a semi-colon in the paragraph of Jewish life has become a huge full stop. Bar/Bat Mitzvah eligibility is still the major impetus for synagogue membership. It can seem like a multi-million pound business.

I teach the course on the Jewish Life Cycle to second-year rabbinic students at Leo Baeck College and enjoy reading many perspectives on the way in which rites of passage form Jewish life. Why do we need rites of passage?

Arnold van Gennep was a French sociologist early last century, fascinated by the way in which different cultures marked growing up. He wrote that every rite of passage is a point of separation from a previous group or situation, then a moment of transition as you cross the threshold leading to incorporation into a new group or situation.[125] When we don't perform that rite of passage the separation and the incorporation don't properly happen. In a Reform Jewish Bat Mitzvah, for example, a young woman leaves the world of the small children of the shul, has a threshold crossing moment in synagogue, reading Torah in front of a community ready to accept her, and is then incorporated into the adult community of our synagogue and the Jewish community as a whole.

The success of what happens is not what takes place on the threshold of course, the reading of Torah, the giving of the D'var Torah, but rather the incorporation into the adult community. You know a Bat Mitzvah or Bar Mitzvah was worthwhile when you meet the young person some years later and they are functioning as a Jewish adult, more learned than they were, participating and contributing to the community, being a Jew.

The ritual of Bar Mitzvah is essentially the same in all branches of Judaism but Bat Mitzvah, the rite of passage for girls, is different in different Jewish movements, due to the extent to which each aims for the girls as women to be incorporated into the adult community on an equal footing to the men. Orthodox Judaism does not currently allow women to read Torah in public, to inhabit what they see as the male spaces of a synagogue, nor to see themselves as bound to the time-based *mitzvot*, the Jewish duties which fall upon a Jewish boy from the age of thirteen. Hence the Orthodox and non-egalitarian variety of Masorti Bat Mitzvah does not include Torah reading, does not take place during the "official" part of the Shabbat morning service nor give the option to the young woman to wear a Tallit, symbolising her acceptance of the *mitzvot*.

---

[125]Quoted in Penina Adelman, 'What Makes a Bat Mitzvah Blossom', in Leonard Greenspoon, ed. *Rites of Passage* (West Lafayette: Purdue University Press, 2010), p2

What we do in Reform synagogues is part of a process of personalisation in which the person is at the centre of the rite of passage rather than the demand of the ritual. But as Rabbi Lawrence Hoffman writes, "when a ritual strays too far from its authorised format it does not feel historically or communally authentic."[126] However, when a traditional ceremony no longer meets the meaning brought to it by its participants, then adaptations to personalise it will come to feel authentic. When a young woman reads from Torah in a Reform synagogue, because our community accepts women as having an equal role in Judaism to men, our community publicly acknowledges that this ceremony, modified from that which takes place in synagogues to the right of Reform in the Jewish spectrum, is indeed rooted in our historical tradition.

As so often, this is a matter of boundaries. A verse in Deuteronomy begins with an unusual feature noticed by the commentator Nachmanides. It starts with the words, "*Shema Yisrael*, Hear O Israel," addressed, you could say, to all Jews as a collective. Then it continues, "*atah over et haYarden,* you are about to pass over the Jordan river."[127] This "you" is in the singular. Meaning that each one of us individually passes over the barriers we need to go through. I love the idea of the Jordan River as the symbol of the barrier which each of us passes through. This is not the Red Sea, which needs a huge collective act of will, or better still a miracle, to get through; that is, it is pretty much insurmountable without divine help. This is the Jordan River which with effort and help any one of us could get through even at its widest points.

That is what a Jewish rite of passage is like. It is do-able. On the one side is a place where you could stay living, the baby boy uncircumcised will still live, the boy or girl who is not Bar or Bat Mitzvah may yet become fully Jewish as an adult, the couple unmarried can have a perfectly happy life together, the person who has died without a funeral will go the way of all flesh. You can stay on the other side of the Jordan. But much better

---

[126] Lawrence Hoffman and Paul Bradshaw eds, *Life Cycles in Jewish and Christian Worship* (University of Notre Dame Press: 1996), p285
[127] Deuteronomy 9:1

for a Jew that you do go through the rite of passage and join the community ready to welcome you and support you on the other side of the spiritual Jordan, as you individually cross the river through your participation in the rite of passage.

That is where my problem is with the Kabbalah Centre Bar Mitzvah, it does not send the young man into the community to welcome him. It is an individual ceremony which actually leaves him nowhere nearer a Jewish community to be with him in his growth. It is why I love the potential of each and every Bar and Bat Mitzvah here at our synagogue. With a good measure of individuality each young person is welcomed into a community which will incorporate their Jewish growth into its own.

# Shabbat Technology?

THERE IS A couple in our community whose son lives in Australia with their daughter-in-law and grandchildren. The couple lives in North West London and their grandchildren are over 10,000 miles away, yet they spend every Shabbat together. Only today's technology makes that possible. When it's nine or ten in the morning in London it's time for Shabbat to begin in Queensland. Their grandchildren light the Shabbat candles in Australia and their grandparents help with the blessings over Skype here in London, every Shabbat.

At every Shabbat service in our synagogue a few people are with us whom we can't see among us. The webcam high up at the back of the synagogue means that a picture of what is happening on the *Bimah*, together with the sound of our voices, is available Friday night and Saturday morning everywhere in the world. It has meant that far-off relatives who were not able to make it to the Bar or Bat Mitzvahs of children in our community have yet been able to be part of the experience and when, for example, a well-known Jewish academic gave a fascinating sermon, his family in Canada and the US were able to hear his words.

For many years a dedicated member of the synagogue has devoted his High Holy Days to ensuring that everyone who wished to, whatever their situation, could be with us for Rosh Hashanah and Yom Kippur. He did this by setting up a webcam to stream the service over the internet, which he monitors and ensures is working through the days. It meant, for example, that in his final weeks a man who had been present for almost every Shabbat and festival service over five decades was able to be with his congregation from a laptop computer on his bed.

Pretty much throughout each High Holy Days at all times more than fifty people are with us through the webcam. This includes family of our members in South Africa and Israel. Members of the synagogue who fall ill on Yom Kippur are able to stay with the services in this way. In years past they would just have missed the spiritual opportunity of the day.

One year we took the possibilities of technology another stage further on Yom Kippur in our family service. More than three hundred parents and children crowded our sanctuary. When we read Torah on Yom Kippur, or anytime in a family service, it is great to enable the children to see the Torah being read and normally I bring them around the reading desk or table. It keeps their attention on it. Much as Moses in his words right after the Ha'azinu poem says, "set these words upon the hearts of your children", there is no better way to make the Torah readings memorable than seeing them being read as well as hearing them.[128]

The trouble is, when we are blessed with so many children around it's not really possible for them all to see as they jostle each other around the table and the little ones, even if they are in the front to see, find not touching the scroll very difficult. So we thought we would try a different way, which I had seen in use at the Union for Reform Judaism convention a couple of years ago in America, Yad Cam. We attached a small high definition camera to the top of the *yad*, which is the hand-shaped pointer we use to read the Torah. This was then connected to a large smart-screen TV. A hugely magnified live picture of the Torah being read word by word was then visible on the screen for all the children at the service, and the adults, too, could engage much more directly with the Torah. I was able to get them reading along with some key phrases and the Torah was truly heard as it was seen.

Now all of these technological possibilities are very effective at making Judaism accessible, but are they right to do on Shabbat or a festival, which is meant to be a day of rest? There is always a *frisson* of disapproval when a phone goes off during a service. Our Youth and Education Department has a policy of not updating its social media on Shabbat

---

[128] Deuteronomy 32:46

during a camp except for safety messages. I do not answer emails on Shabbat. With this and many examples, we as Reform Jews continue to observe the prohibition on using electrical devices on Shabbat and festivals.

The reasons for this prohibition are rooted in the basis of Shabbat observance in the Book of Exodus; "Six days shall work be done, but on the seventh day there shall be to you a holy day, a Shabbat of rest to the Eternal; whoever does work in it shall be put to death. You shall kindle no fire throughout your habitations upon the Sabbath day."[129]

Jewish communities do not put anybody to death for Shabbat observance violations but we absolutely do try to find our way to enjoy a Shabbat of rest. The definition of that rest is where different groups of Jews have different interpretations. From the prohibition of fire, Jews who follow classical Rabbinic interpretation assume that once a fire is lit it can stay lit on the Shabbat, a light once on, or an oven once lit, can stay lit.

Two groups which do not follow Rabbinic interpretative traditions, the Karaites (of whom there are still around 40,000 worldwide) and the Samaritans (of whom there are around 1,000 in the world), with different interpretations of Israelite traditions, both assume that there should be no benefit from fire or its derivative, electricity, throughout Shabbat. This meant that when Samaritan elder Beny Sedaka came to visit and speak at our synagogue on Shabbat he had to stay in his bedroom from five in the afternoon till dawn so that he was not benefitting from the electricity used by his hosts.

For most Jews who observe the Shabbat by current rabbinic law, it is the completion of a new circuit that they avoid. They work on the basis that this prohibition is derived from one of the pieces of work, known as *melachot*, forbidden on Shabbat, of which making a fire is an example.

---

[129] Exodus 35:2

They were first set out in the Mishnah Shabbat in the second century CE.[130]

How does Reform Judaism deal with the idea of there being forbidden tasks on Shabbat? We aim to enjoy a Shabbat and festival of rest, where coming together for worship and then togetherness untroubled by day to day concerns is key week after week. Where we differ from other more strict interpretations of the thrust of Jewish law is on the definition of the *melachot*, the work that needs to be avoided in order for that rest to take place. The original definitions of the thirty-nine *melachot* to be avoided on the Shabbat were based on the tasks that would be needed for equipping the Tabernacle, the desert temple, the great symbol of Israelite God-guided creativity in the Torah. These works of construction, making, food production, were subsequently extended as technology was introduced, so that car driving and making new electric circuits became part of the prohibitions.

What we do, though, in allowing and indeed encouraging the use of electric technology is not against the spirit of the *melachot*. We still say that a Shabbat or festival of rest can only be achieved if we leave off these pieces of everyday work, my favoured definition of the word *melachah*. Not using the phone for business, letting your social media presence rest, doing activities which bring people together rather than putting them in front of technology. But we are also comfortable with the use of technology to enable people to be part of a Shabbat or festival of rest.

Technology for inclusion, such as the webcam or Yad Cam, feels right to me. It brings us together to celebrate Shabbat or to engage in a festival. We will always be skirting at the limits and we have to continue the Talmudic process of working out just where these lie. Reform Judaism leaves "maybe" open. We as a community have to decide where "maybe" becomes "yes" or "no."

---

[130] Mishnah Shabbat 7:2

# Jewish Society

# Our Ketubah With Society

EVERY YEAR OUR synagogue is blessed with many weddings. Most are couples where one of the partners grew up in the community, though some are couples who found us by recommendation. Each wedding takes quite a bit of work on the part of the rabbi or cantor who is officiating, meeting up, working out just how the couple will gain most meaning from the Jewish ritual, talking about married life and the potential of a Jewish couple to build a Jewish home, working out the music and, now taking more and more work than it used to, creating the ketubah, the Jewish marriage contract.

It used to be that most couples simply used the ketubah that the Movement for Reform Judaism provided. We shared its content with the couples, they felt fine that what was within it applied to them and the ketubah was duly prepared for the big day. Not any more, or at least not often.

The men and women who want to get married through our synagogue are becoming ever more assertive about what they would like to see written in their ketubah and most weddings now require the actually quite delightful task of negotiating the text of this document. Three factors are to blame or to credit for this phenomenon. One is the Anita Diamant book, *The New Jewish Wedding*, which most empowered Jewish couples bring to their rabbi, full of ideas as to how to make their ceremony and the ketubah which records it special. The second factor is the work of many Jewish artists who market ketubot, especially created, and will offer a variety of wordings to include on them. The third factor, though, is that today's couples marrying through a Reform synagogue have normally been living in very close contact for some years. They are, of course, not couples who were introduced to each other a short time before their wedding by their respective families and told that they had better marry each other.

Reform Jewish couples have often been living together for months if not years before they decide to marry and so they know each other very well. The impersonal words of a standard ketubah do not feel appropriate to govern their marriage. The standard Reform ketubah is based around a promise to cherish and support each other according to the law of Moses and Israel and then to build a Jewish home among the people of Israel. The promise is witnessed by those around them at the wedding ceremony. The standard Orthodox ketubah is based around a similar promise backed up by a guarantee to keep the amount of the bride's dowry (actual or imaginary) safe for return to her in the case of divorce. And that's what the problem is. Neither sounds terribly romantic nor relevant to the years of love and companionship which the couple is hoping to enjoy together.

So I have been working with couples on trying to ensure that in the ketubot they create which speak about hearts being united and full of tenderness, hope and wonder, doing everything within their power to permit each of them to become the persons they are yet to be, challenging each other to achieve intellectual and physical fulfilment as we search for spiritual and emotional peace and being ever open while cherishing each other's uniqueness, there is also the appropriate Jewish content. The thoughts are lovely, though I suspect rather difficult to enforce in a Beit Din, Jewish law court, which is the ultimate sanction for failing to uphold the terms of a ketubah. They occasionally create some chuckles when, as they must be, they are read out at a wedding. I remember in particular one clause in a ketubah which promised that neither bride nor groom would ever enter their home with impatience or anger which had many longer-married couples among the congregation looking at each other with knowing glances which I reckon said, "I'll give that idea six months top."

The ketubah is there because Judaism is a religion based on a contract, a covenant, which the ketubah models. The final terms of this contract are read each year in synagogue as we reach the end of the Books of Leviticus and Deuteronomy.[131] The Torah, before we reach these points, has been full of hope for the future, invoking a society where workers will be paid on time, where no-one will sell on false measures, where God, not us, will own the land, where we will not steal nor swear falsely, where we will love our neighbours as ourselves. In the last portion of the Book of Leviticus we hear what will happen if we do observe it all – a society of fairness and prosperity, comfort and co-operation – and what will happen if we do not observe it – a disaster of a society where everything goes wrong in a house-of-cards-like sequence leading to exile and even starvation as everyone grabs what they think is theirs until in turn they have it grabbed away from them.

The opening words of the last Torah portion of the Book of Leviticus show that Judaism is neither a religion of optimism nor pessimism. The portion opens with the words "*im bechukkotai telech,* if you follow my laws". Judaism is a religion of "if-ism", our actions have consequences and we have to take responsibility for them, just as it says in our ketubot.[132]

If our society is narrow, uncaring, self-interested and unequal, then we will have to live with being constricted ourselves behind barriers, with having to fend for ourselves when we are in hard times, with the causes of troubles not being addressed and with the potential to be at the bottom of a hierarchical heap. If our society is open, concerned, involved with the lives of all and with a structure giving equality of opportunity, then we will have our own freedom, be helped when we need it, address the problems that will inevitably be there and have the chance for all to thrive. "If-ism" is the natural consequence of living in covenant with God.

We live in contract with each other as much as a married couple lives in a contract formed by their ketubah. Our Torah says we also live in a contract with God. So whenever we are empowered to spell out the terms

---

[131] Leviticus 26:3-46 and Deuteronomy Chapter 28
[132] Levicitcus 26:3 – this interpretation was first made by Rabbi Mordechai Kaplan

of that contract we need to take that power and ensure that it is done in accordance with our Jewish values. This happens every time we are given the chance to vote. To me not voting is like coming to a marriage contract and saying that you are willing to let your partner set all of the terms. You will sign at the bottom accepting a long-term relationship with a political party but couldn't care less what the terms of that relationship will be. A covenant people, which lives by "if", should not do that Perhaps it is why Israeli democracy is so vital, even if impossible.

We must have a stake in the terms under which our society is built. So a Jew should vote in every election in which we are entitled. Our synagogue is not party political. Yet as we work with couples to include the terms **they** need in their ketubah, so a thriving synagogue is willing to debate the terms on which our society is built, but does not see the synagogue as a place where those terms should be monolithically established on party lines. In a General Election we will host a hustings but all parties will be there.

There is a line, though, which must not be crossed. That is where racism is part of the apparent appeal of a party. The people of whom it was said by the *Manchester City News* in 1888, "These immigrants have flooded the labour market with cheap labour to such an extent as to reduce thousands of native workers to the verge of destitution." The people of whom the *Sunday Express* wrote in 1938, "Just now there is a big influx of foreigners into Britain. They are overrunning the country. They are trying to enter the medical profession in great numbers. Worst of all, many of them are holding themselves out to the public as psychoanalysts." This people cannot be involved in a politics which says, as the former UKIP leader Nigel Farage did, "I would not want to live next to Romanians," or that another European people "is raised in a culture of criminality."[133] There is a line which the Jewish covenant says a society must never cross. There are terms in our contract with each other which can never appropriately be in our ketubah.

---

[133] *The Guardian*, 19 May 2014

# When The Wilderness Is Good For You

WHEN I NEED to write a sermon or an article, and as a rabbi I often do, I find that the thing I really need to get started is space. It is very difficult for me to write with quality in a busy synagogue office, to enjoy the free flow of ideas and connections that enables a sermon to take people on a journey that is worth participating in. So my most effective way of writing a sermon is to spend time gathering ideas and research on the texts which feel meaningful to a portion, and then get on my bike or into a swimming pool. Then I can find the space, no music, no more reading, just the space to think and freely associate what I have been learning. It is wonderfully effective just to find the space, to step into the wilderness until something worth communicating begins to build in the space that is left. I am sure that I share this need with many.

The formation of the Jewish people takes place in the wilderness, as we begin to receive Torah. Mechilta de Rabbi Ishmael (to Exodus 19:2) asks why Torah was not given once the people had crossed the Jordan and were ready to establish their society of Israel. Why was it not given in a grand palace? Why was it not given on the highest mountain or once a Temple had been built? The Midrash answers: "The Torah was given in public, openly in a free place. For had the Torah been given in the land of Israel, the Israelites could have said to the nations of the world: 'You have no share in it.' But now that it was given in the wilderness publicly and openly in a place that is free to all, everyone wishing to accept it could come and accept it."[134] It was in the open space of the wilderness, *bemidbar*, that the people could receive and engage with the radical ideas which were to form them.

The same happened with Moses's call. He was called to be a leader, to hear God not in Pharaoh's palace, not at the sacrificial site which we can

---

[134] Mechilta de Rabbi Ishmael to Exodus 19:2

assume that his Midianite priest father-in-law Jethro must have kept, but in blank space, in the wilderness where he was tending his sheep, when he was able to open his eyes and perceive that the bush was burning and that a message was being called out to him.[135]

When Moses sings his last song at the end of the Book of Deuteronomy, *Ha'azinu*, he makes it clear how important the space of the wilderness was for the encounter of God and the Jewish people to begin. "For God's portion is his people; Jacob is the lot of his inheritance. He found him in a desert land, and in the waste, a howling wilderness; He led him about, he instructed him, He kept him as the apple of his eye."[136] The people would not have been open to the instruction if they had not come out of the narrow life they led in Egypt into the space of the wilderness.

We all need space to learn and to be creative and to respond to the wonder of God's world. The final chapters of the Book of Leviticus establish that once the Children of Israel reached the Promised Land they would be required to grant themselves space, times of wilderness in their lives. The rest of the book had been filled with instructions for making the *Mishcan*, the desert sanctuary, work, and then for making their society work, very busy chapters. But there is to be a system for finding space. Firstly, every week one day is to be Shabbat, a time when the everyday demands of work and busyness are set aside so that every Jew has time to value their very existence and their God-given humanity. Secondly, every seventh year is to be a *Shmittah* year, a year when the regular agricultural activity ceases and the people live off the natural bounty of the land, giving space to the land to recover and changing busyness into calmness. Thirdly, every forty-ninth year the whole land is restored by another year of rest, the *Yovel*, or Jubilee year.[137] Everything that had been gained by pushy economic activity is restored to its former owners so that the whole society spends a year effectively

---

[135] Exodus 3:2ff
[136] Deuteronomy 32:9-10
[137] Leviticus Chapters 23-25

in the wilderness in their own land, restoring the God-given balance to their society.

Though these structures of rest and space were given in the Torah, it has always been tempting not to observe them. Our lives, it seems, can always be more productive if we never stop. Our wealth, it seems, can be greater if we never restore balance in our society between the rich and the poor. Our assets can always be more intensively used, all at the cost of the real value of our lives. The existence of the Book of Jubilees in the collection of our ancient extra-biblical texts suggests very strongly that the Jubilee year of release every forty-nine years was simply not observed. Many powerful people in Israelite society had a vested interest in balance never being restored. The *Shmittah* or Sabbatical year of lying fallow was widely enough observed for it to be commented upon by the Roman Jewish historian Josephus as surprising to the Romans, who thought it a very strange way to run an economy. Yet many Israelites ceased to make loans to each other when the year was approaching, since those loans would become unrepayable and the strong language at the end of the Book of Leviticus about what would happen if the Sabbatical years were not observed hints that non-observance was common. Why warn against something if it was not happening?

It is also tempting to keep working through Shabbat. Not to give ourselves one day a week when we restore ourselves as full people.

What is the cost of failing to give ourselves space? Claude Montefiore put it beautifully when he wrote: "There are objects in life higher than success. The Sabbath, with its exhortation to the worship of God and the doing of kindly deeds, reminds us week by week of these higher objects. It prevents us reducing our life to the level of a machine."[138]

A wilderness, to be bearable for any length of time, needs, perhaps counterintuitively, a sense of structure amid the space. As we enter the

---

[138] Claude Montefiore, *The Bible for Home Reading*, Part 1, p88

Book of Numbers, the Children of Israel begin to organise their encampment. Each tribe is numbered, they are put into an order or formation, the camp is organised, the Levite clans are each given their tasks. They are made ready to move on towards the Promised Land.[139] So too, our times of rest, of wilderness, are made more meaningful by structure. The Jubilee year was meant to be accompanied by an organised re-assignment of land to its original tribal holders. The Sabbatical *Shmittah* year should include the release of all slaves, and the cancellation of all loans. The Shabbat day is structured by prayer and learning together with a community. There is space and rest but that rest is made meaningful by a certain degree of structure.

Written into the contracts of all the rabbis of my synagogue is the requirement to stop work on behalf of the synagogue for three months at the end of three years, so that we can restore our creativity and so that we can study without interruption. For three months my regular duties to be on hand at all times for the needs of the members of the synagogue, to teach, to lead and to manage are set aside as we are granted some time to be in the wilderness. This is a far- sighted gift by the synagogue Council to the members of the synagogue because it ensures that rabbis do not depreciate in value with every passing year, but rather have time to build themselves so that they can give more in learning and quality of practice, just as the rested land from the Sabbatical year has time to gather nutrients in order to create better harvests in the future. Sabbaticals also help rabbinic families to cope with the pressures and demands of this profession by giving quality time back at least for a period. Most of us give our sabbaticals structure so that in that time we know that we have achieved something of substance. We all need space to grow, to think and to learn.

---

[139] Numbers Chapters 2-4

# The Everlasting Congregation Does Not Exist

I HAVE A particular technique when I am hosting a school visit to a synagogue. Judaism is currently on the National Curriculum for Year 3 children so I have hosted many visits from schools local to the synagogues where I have been Rabbi. The children are often on a series of visits to local churches, mosques, temples and shuls. I bring the children into the sanctuary and ask them to sit down. Then I ask them to close their eyes and imagine that they are in a bare hall, just chairs, a bare floor, walls and ceiling. After thirty seconds or so I ask them to open their eyes and to tell me what they can see that makes the room in which they are a synagogue and not just any hall.

If I am lucky there will be a forest of enthusiastic hands. The children will notice the *Bimah*, the Ark or *Aron HaKodesh*, the Hebrew above the Ark and the *Ner Tamid*, each one worthy of explanation and giving us a starting point for making the visit meaningful. Sometimes I make myself a hostage to fortune and ask them what they think the objects they can see are, so that they can display their previous classroom learning.

I don't always get the answer I am hoping for! Once, when I asked a class what they thought was inside the Ark, I received a chorus back from children who were obviously getting confused as to which place of worship they were in: "The idols".

The *Ner Tamid* always inspires interest – because I say that it is an everlasting light. To the eight-year-old mind this is a description worthy of challenge. Some child will always ask, "Does it ever go out? What do you do if you need to change the bulb?" Eventually they come to be satisfied with its symbolic value, but those practical questions have to be answered.

The *Ner Tamid* at our synagogue has a history. Children at the Sunday religion school in the earliest years of the synagogue used to bring in a penny a week for the *Ner Tamid* fund, which paid for the everlasting light. Children, who are now in their eighties and nineties, lit the lamp themselves.

It was originally bare copper, now overlaid to preserve it, and it was designed and made by Benno Elkan, the sculptor who made the famous Menorah depicting the story of the Jews given to the Knesset in Jerusalem by the British Parliament. The words around the outside of the *Ner Tamid* are from the Book of Proverbs: '*Ner Adonai Nishmat Adam*, The soul of every person is the Light of God.'[140]

We are used to calling these lamps, which can be seen in every synagogue around the world, by the name *Ner Tamid*, everlasting light, as if it were a term in common use forever. Actually, in the Torah the words *Ner* and *Tamid* are not written as a single phrase. If you are familiar with the notes that accompany the Torah portion, the *neginot*, you notice that on the two occasions when the words *Ner* and *Tamid* come together in a sentence in the Torah they are written *l'ha'alot ner tamid,* to be chanted like this: "*merchah tipchah sof pasuk.*" *L'ha'alot ner* goes together, while *tamid,* as you can hear when it is chanted, is a separate word.[141]

Now, whilst the notes which are used to chant the portion did not exist in fixed notation until only fifteen hundred years ago or so, they are based on age-old orally transmitted traditions of how the Torah portions were sung in our synagogues. So what were our ancestor rabbis trying to emphasise in this choice of musical phrase? Not that *Ner* and *Tamid* went together, but that *l'haalot* and *ner* go together. *L'haalot* means "to light" or "to kindle". *Ner* is the noun form for light. This means that *l'haalot ner tamid* does not mean kindle an "everlasting light" but kindle a light

---

140 Proverbs 20:27
141 Exodus 27:20 and Leviticus 24:2

continually. That is how it is translated in most versions of the Torah. *Tamid* is translated "continually", "constantly" or "regularly."

So that light in front of our Ark is not an everlasting light but rather it is a light which by our efforts we keep burning. Indeed, in the *mi she'berach* for the community, the words of blessing for the whole congregation said in the traditional Shabbat service after the Torah reading, among the people for whom God's blessing is asked are those who provide the lamps for illuminating the synagogue. It is a constant task.

Once in the history of our synagogue's *Ner Tamid*, keeping our synagogue lamp alight continually was physically a constant task. Right now there is a convenient electric cord running down the chains supporting the *Ner Tamid*, but when it was first installed here, through the contributions of the synagogue's first cheder children, it was fuelled by oil. So it remained in the early days of the congregation, until the effort required to refill the oil was replaced with the convenience of electricity, sometime in the late '50s or early '60s.

You look at that *Ner Tamid* and it is easy to imagine that little needs to go into keeping the light burning. It is just there. But no congregation is an everlasting congregation. A congregation needs to be tended continually. It is the responsibility of all members of a synagogue congregation, *mitzvah* even, to join those who keep the light burning and so earn for ourselves the blessing of one who illuminates the synagogue over the coming years.

When those school visits happen children often ask what the *Ner Tamid* is for, what it actually represents. As so often in Judaism, there are many perfectly valid interpretations. Some say it is to represent God's dwelling in our sanctuaries as once God's spirit dwelt in the *Mishkan*, the original desert sanctuary which was the prototype for the Temple.[142] Some say

---

[142] Exodus 25:8

that it represents the refusal of Judaism to die out whatever challenges, pressures and oppression we are put under. The Rabbis say that that is why olive oil was used to light *nerot*, because the clarity of flame that it produces can only be obtained by pressing and grinding the olives almost into submission, and why light is the symbol of Jewish survival at Chanukkah.[143] But also the light represents the light of Judaism in every person who belongs to a synagogue, a light that can reach out to anyone who will visit any synagogue in the future.

---

[143] Midrash Exodus Rabbah 36:1

# Women Rabbis

IN 1975 JAQUELINE TABICK was ordained as a rabbi. She went on to serve for more than two decades as a rabbi at the West London Synagogue and then for more than a decade as the rabbi of the North West Surrey Synagogue and is currently the Head of the Movement for Reform Judaism Beit Din. Over forty years ago Rabbi Tabick, who was then single and called Jaqueline Acker, applied to train for the rabbinate at Leo Baeck College.

Her application was duly acknowledged, but the acknowledgement was addressed to a Mr Acker, not to Miss Acker, as Jackie correctly was. An inordinate delay ensued in giving Jacqueline, who was to become the first woman rabbi in Britain, an interview. But eventually it was arranged. Unlike all the male applicants of that year, who included Rabbi Cliff Cohen and Rabbi Stephen Katz, Jackie Acker was tested on her ability to read and understand Mishnah, the assumption apparently being made that, as a woman, she would be unlikely to have sufficient Hebrew skills.

All went fine for Jackie at the College. She was duly ordained in 1975 to be a rabbi, by this time married to Larry Tabick, who received Semichah the following year. Jackie's first position as a rabbi required a little, shall we say, finessing. She was employed as the Educational Director of the West London Synagogue not as Rabbi or even Assistant Rabbi, both of which would have required validation at the synagogue's Annual General Meeting, and many of us will be aware of what happens when otherwise sensible recruitment decisions are brought to AGMs.

A few times, Jackie has written, she has been irritated by the absurdity surrounding her being the first British woman rabbi. For example, when pictures were taken by the press at her ordination, Rabbi Tabick insisted that all the ordinands, male and female, were in the shots. But then when they were printed in the press all the others were cropped from the pictures so that they reported only the ordination of her as a woman! Another press-inspired irritation was when she was phoned by a *Jewish Chronicle* reporter to ask what she, as a woman rabbi, thought about current bridal fashion.

In recent years an average intake year for Leo Baeck College has been 50/50 men and women, so it won't be long until the British Progressive Rabbinate, Liberal and Reform, approaches parity between men and women. Currently, over a third of rabbis serving congregations in the British Movement for Reform Judaism and Liberal Judaism are women.

It has often been suggested that women rabbis must make a particular contribution to the rabbinate because they are women. This suggestion is normally based on stereotypes of feminine characteristics and skills. The assumption is made that women rabbis must necessarily be better at pastoral care, less able to work within synagogue power structures, better at co-operative and team efforts within community life but unable to dedicate themselves fully to the job due to childcare responsibilities. It takes only a few minutes thinking through the current members of the British rabbinate who are women to dispel these stereotypes. But in Jackie Tabick we have a rabbi who was very effective in enabling West London to offer the full facilities of a community synagogue as well as its cathedral status and now leads the Reform Beit Din. In Rabbi Baroness Julia Neuberger, who was ordained just a few years after Jackie, we have a rabbi who demonstrates continually in her own work how Judaism incorporates social and political action into our religious principles. In Rabbi Sybil Sheridan, with over thirty years' service in the rabbinate, we have an author and editor of several of the source books of modern Progressive Judaism, including *Hear Our Voice*, the collected works of Britain's women rabbis, and *Taking up the Timbrel*, a collection on innovative Jewish ritual. The Senior Rabbi to the Movement for Reform Judaism is Rabbi Laura Janner-Klausner. Each of them has contributed to British Jewish life as rabbis. That they are women is almost irrelevant to the contribution that they make except that they act as role models to other able young women to put themselves forward as potential leaders of the Jewish community.

It is undoubted, however, that the advent of women rabbis, along with complementary trends in society in general, has helped us to rediscover the women in the Bible and Talmud and in Jewish history in general, and to be more open to ritual which reflects the reality of family life, such as services for unborn children and neo-nates. Also their presence has helped to inspire Orthodox Jewish women to begin to test the boundaries that Orthodoxy continues to put on women's religious participation.

There is, though, still some residual prejudice against women rabbis. Much of it is emotionally based and only takes some time spent witnessing the work of a real woman rabbi to dispel. There was a man at Jackie Tabick's Weybridge Synagogue who, when she was about to be appointed, said, "No way to a woman rabbi." Once she had been appointed he changed to, "OK, provided she does not do my funeral"; then, after a few months, on to, "She can give the eulogy but not lead the service." After a year or so he said, "She can do it all."

Some of those who are unsure about the idea of a woman rabbi are concerned that the whole idea is against Jewish tradition. For them I think that it is important to understand why the woman rabbi has not been seen before recent times. It is based on the idea that a woman should not be taught Torah, that essential to Jewish instruction which is the basic toolbox of the rabbi. Why not? Because it says in Deuteronomy that "You shall teach these words of Torah to your children"; in Hebrew, *v'limad'tem otam et bneichem*.[144] *Bneichem*, children, we would assume means girls and boys, but that is not how it was taken by the strand of rabbinic opinion that took women out of Torah study, though be aware that they only exempted women from studying Torah. They did not ban them.

---

[144] Deuteronomy 11:19

Those rabbis decided that in this occurrence of the word *bnei* it would mean sons, boy-children only, not of course how they understood it in the phrase *Bnei Yisrael*, where it is always Children of Israel. When the text refers to children and wants to make a distinction between girls and boys, Moses deliberately splits it up into *b'vaneinu u'vivnoteinu*, our sons and our daughters.[145]

So when the rabbis chose to take *b'neichem* in the Deuteronomy verse, and you shall teach Torah to your children, to mean sons only, they did just that. They made a choice. This choice was obviously based on the societal norms of their time, when women were not educated in the same way as men, when different things were expected of them, when in the second century CE, in the Mishnah, Rabbi Eliezer was able to say that, "The sages command that a father not teach Torah to his daughter, for most women are not intellectually suited to learn. Rather, due to their lack of intelligence, they are liable to interpret the words of Torah in vain and foolish ways."[146]

As long as one knows that the assumptions behind this statement and others are false, scientifically and socially unsupportable, then a Reform Jew, who should interpret halachah, Jewish law, in the light of their ethical conscience and modern knowledge, cannot hold to the idea that a woman is by her gender unsuitable to be a rabbi.

Indeed it was back in 1922 that the Central Conference of American Rabbis, the rabbinic authority of the American Reform movement, declared that it could see no reason why a woman should not train to become a rabbi, although it took until 1972 for Sally Preisland to be ordained as the first American woman rabbi. In the Liberal Jewish movement Lily Montagu served as a *de facto* minister from 1918, when she first delivered a sermon at the Liberal Jewish Synagogue in St John's Wood. She served then as Lay Minister of the West Central Liberal Synagogue virtually from its foundation onwards. There was a woman

---

[145] Exodus 10:9
[146] Mishnah Sotah 3:4

rabbi ordained within the German Liberale movement, Regina Jonas, who was ordained by Rabbi Leo Baeck himself in 1942. She served a congregation in Frankfurt. Rabbi Regina Jonas was murdered in the Shoah.[147]

This brings us to the position nowadays, when gender has no effect whatsoever on one's chances of being accepted on the rabbinic programme of Leo Baeck College or its US counterpart, Hebrew Union College. Though I know well that women rabbis may be going out into a synagogue world where, whilst synagogues which have employed a woman rabbi might ask themselves, should we have a woman rabbi again, no synagogue that I know of asks whether it is on for a male rabbi to succeed another male rabbi. It is also a world where women are grossly underrepresented in national and regional Jewish leadership. American studies continue to show a substantial pay gap between the average for male and female rabbis.[148] Being a woman rabbi is undoubtedly more personally challenging than being a male rabbi.

I hope that in their Jewish lives our children will continue to grow more and more confident in women's equal participation in Judaism. I hope that they see it as normative and that they recognise that those parts of Judaism which restrict women's participation are doing so out of choices made in the past which are overlaid with human social values rather than a real response to God. At the time of the seventh plague Pharaoh offered Moses the opportunity to leave Egypt just with the men. He refused. There is no real Jewish community until men and women embark on the journey of creating and sustaining Jewish life together.[149]

---

[147] Borts, Barbara and Tikvah Sarah, Elli, *Women Rabbis in the Pulpit* (London: Kulmus, 2015), pp24-25, includes a fuller account of women who studied at rabbinic seminaries or served in rabbinic roles
[148] www.jta.org/2016/05/31/life-religion/why-a-small-word-change-is-a-big-deal-for-reform-women-rabbis
[149] Exodus 10:9

# Finding The Perfect Rabbi

I WAS A student rabbi for a year at the Liberal Jewish Synagogue in St John's Wood, London. Student rabbis at that august synagogue were allowed to use Rabbi John Rayner's office to put on their robes and tallit before leading services. As a kind of encouragement to us there was a framed poster on the wall of the office. It was entitled "The Perfect Rabbi" and described the kind of rabbinate that we Leo Baeck College students should surely aim to live up to:

"The perfect rabbi's sermons last for exactly twelve minutes. The perfect rabbi condemns sin, but never upsets anyone. He works from 8:00 a.m. until midnight and his spare time hobby is being a synagogue janitor. He is happy to be paid $50 a week, wears good clothes, buys good books, drives a good car, and gives about $50 weekly to the poor. The perfect rabbi is 28 years old and has the benefit of 30 years' experience in the Rabbinate. He has a burning desire to work with teenagers and spends all his time with senior citizens. The perfect rabbi smiles all the time with a straight face because he has a sense of humour that keeps him seriously dedicated to his work. He makes 15 calls daily on congregational families, the housebound and the hospitalized and is always in his office when you call him."

I think that we can agree that the perfect rabbi does not exist.

For five years, from 1998 to 2003, I had the task of Eliezer, Abraham's servant. Eliezer's job was to find the perfect wife for his master's son, Isaac, from among Abraham's own tribe. Does the perfect partner exist?

Abraham said to Eliezer, "You'll know when you see her – she will be just the right woman and will follow you willingly back to Isaac." After a few days' journey Eliezer found Rebekah. She was truly a remarkable woman. How do we know? Because when Eliezer, the stranger, met her at the well, she single-handedly gave water to his ten camels.[150] Big deal?

Yes it is when you know that the average camel drinks fifteen gallons of water. That's more than sixty litres in one sitting.[151] That means that the Rebekah whom Eliezer found was strong enough to pull a sizeable bucket up from a well fifty to sixty times, and all this just for a man whom she took to be a visiting stranger. Strong and stunning too, at least that was Isaac's reaction when he saw her for the first time as she approached near to where he was meditating in the field.

My task for those five years was not to find the perfect *shidduch*, marriage partner, for a notional Isaac, but rather to find *shidduchin* for the synagogues of the UK, as I worked for a half a day a week as Leo Baeck College's Rabbinic Recruitment Officer.

You may wonder why Leo Baeck College needed a Rabbinic Recruitment Officer. Surely the rabbinic selection process begins in, shall we say, a higher place? That has never been the view of Judaism. The rabbi has always been someone who, it is hoped, by virtue of their learning, leadership skills, community involvement and commitment, earns the respect of those whom they serve. Indeed, one of the points of contrast between Judaism and Christianity is that rabbis, in theory at least, need not hear, so to speak, the voice of the Almighty calling them to work, whilst priests are, by definition, people who are convinced of their vocation to offer themselves as shepherds to God's flock.

Of course in reality this contrast is not so clear-cut. A priest with a strong vocation but little learning, leadership skills, community-feel and commitment is likely to have an awful time with their congregation, whilst a rabbi needs the reassurance that God supports them in their work to deal with the inevitable difficulties and demands of congregational life.

---

[150] Genesis 24:20
[151] *Journal of Camel Science*, 2004, 1: pp66-70

In Jewish understanding, the Almighty ceased to engage in direct recruitment work once the age of prophecy ceased with Malachi. Furthermore, the Almighty made only one direct rabbinic appointment, that of Moshe Rabbenu, Moses, whose leadership, as our Torah tells us, was just as much up for question by the people whom he led as that of any modern rabbi. So much for the authority that a strong sense of vocation might be thought to give you. Therefore there has always been a more or less informal means of rabbinic recruitment, from the promotion of the disciples of the rabbis of old to succeed their masters as the interpreters of our scriptures, to the support that communities gave to their talented youngsters to enter yeshivot (Jewish institutes of higher learning), to the mentoring of likely people by a rabbi who, so to speak, talent-spots them, something at which Rabbis Lionel Blue, Hugo Gryn, Werner Van der Zyl, Andrew Goldstein and Sheila Shulman, are, or have been, most adept.

The more formal approach of there being a Leo Baeck College Rabbinic Recruitment Officer came about due to a change in the Jewish life pattern of committed Jewish young people. In past years they grew up with a particular synagogue and then stayed in relationship with that or another synagogue through youth clubs, young marrieds' groups, etc. Nowadays, our most committed young people end up identifying more with the national Jewish youth movements, RSY-Netzer and LJY-Netzer, than with their own synagogue and its rabbi. For this reason the level of contact, rabbi to young person, is not as great as it once was. There had been a distinct shortage of our own young people coming forward to train for the rabbinate.

Year after year now there has been a shortage of rabbis for the pulpits available, and with a wave of retirements of the rabbis who trained in the '60s and early '70s well under way, this shortage will only increase. That was why Leo Baeck College decided to do something proactive, and try to create a bridge between the Youth Movements and Leo Baeck College through activities such as Shadow a Rabbi Day, Learning for

Jewish Life Seminars, and workshops entitled "Have you ever considered becoming a rabbi" at Movement events.

What kind of career does the rabbinate offer? To me it is one which probably offers more personal fulfilment than any other possible career. As a rabbi one is able to give expression to pretty much any skill that you have. If you can sing then you sing. If you enjoy teaching then you teach. If you are academically inclined then study and write. If you love people then you will find yourself taken into their lives in a most privileged way. If there is something of the performer in you the rabbinate gives you plenty of opportunity. If you enjoy working in a team, then what is a congregation but a giant team working towards the Messianic Age? I am not blind to the downsides of the rabbinate, in particular the difficulties of leading a full family life whilst being, in theory, on call at all times to thousands of people.

The rabbinate into which we should aim to draw the most talented, committed Jews is one whose nature has fundamentally changed over the past decades. The Talmud tells us, "Like generation, like leader".[152] So as our society has changed its patterns of working and, in particular, has questioned the need for hierarchy, we rabbis, like so many Christian priests, have cast off our preaching robes, or in my case and that of most of my contemporaries, never put them on, and tried to remove the barriers of authority which we felt were keeping us away from the people whom we were aiming to serve. We have tried to be less figures of authority and more empowerers, relying not upon the mystique of our position to give us the authority we need in order to function, but rather upon the earning of respect. Much as religion can no longer call upon people in contemporary society with the confidence that it is seen as necessary, pretty much all Jews and all Christians nowadays make a positive choice in their lives actually to practice and put any store by their religion. So to do they make a positive choice whether or not to respect their rabbi, priest or minister.

---

[152] Babylonian Talmud Arachin 17a

In the Talmud, Rabbi Isaac said, "A leader is not to be appointed unless the community is first consulted."[153] Whilst taking this aphorism too literally can have uncomfortable and unfortunate results, as happened in years gone by in various synagogues, a rabbi cannot nowadays become a leader just by virtue of their title. They need to be able to take a community with them – in the words of Zechariah, "Not by might, not by power but by spirit."[154] Today's rabbi needs to call up the spirit of co-operation, of shared mission for a synagogue, of excitement at the adventure that is the creation of a thriving Jewish community.

It is a tough role that we ask nowadays of our rabbis, combining many different and even contradictory skills and qualities. We ask them to be studious and yet extrovert, to be a personal guide and *confidant* and yet to exert authority in a community, to build a community and yet to work outside the definitions of success used in businesses, to give deep thought to actions and words and yet to engage in a bewildering variety of activities every day.

What we need to do every year, rabbis and lay people together, is to encourage people who could succeed in any walk of life to consider putting their talents and commitment into service to the Jewish community as its next generation of rabbis.

---

[153] Babylonian Talmud Berachot 55a
[154] Zechariah 4:6

# Every Life Has Its Ups And Downs

THE AGES THAT people live to in the early chapters of the Torah get a bit crazy. Noah is, according to the Torah, 600 years old when he leaves the ark, and he then goes on to live to 950 years of age. Noah, though, does not live the longest life in the Torah. The greatest age was attained by Methuselah, who enjoyed 969 years of life before succumbing to his mortality.[155]

Things calm down once we reach the Torah era of Abraham, as if to tell us that we are leaving legendary time and coming closer to our own era of a lifespan determined by the limitations of our physiology. The first death in Abraham's own family recorded in Torah is that of Sarah, wife of Abraham, mother of Isaac and founder of Judaism.

Sarah dies, we are told, at "just" 127 years of age.[156] From now on no-one in the Bible lives for more than 175 years and, once we leave Genesis, the longest life is that of Moses at 120 years. This is the origin of the Jewish greeting of good wishes, *ud mea v esrim* (may you live to 120) which turned in English to our greeting to mourners, "I wish you long life." The longest medically documented life ever lived was that of Jeanne Calment who died in 1997 at the age of 122. So with Moses we leave the stuff of legends where age is concerned and stay in physiological reality for the rest of the Bible.

Why did Sarah die? After all, the Rabbis say that the opening words of the portion, stating that she lived for 127 years, tell us that at one hundred Sarah was as vigorous and beautiful as a woman of twenty, and that at twenty she had been as innocent and sweet as a girl of seven.[157]

---

[155] Genesis 5:27
[156] Genesis 23:1
[157] Midrash Genesis Rabbah 58:1

Midrash explains that she died not from a physical cause but from the extremes of grief that she suffered as a result of what had happened in the chapter just before Sarah's death is recorded, the *Akedah,* or binding of Isaac.[158] The Midrash notes that from the moment that Abraham packed up the donkey with firewood, his knife and a fire lantern and took Isaac off to a faraway mountain to sacrifice him we do not hear Sarah mentioned again until we hear of her death. She never knew that the sacrifice had not happened and that Isaac returned unharmed to the family encampment in Beer Sheva. Through the mental anguish of her grief, she died.[159]

There is an undercurrent of distress and disturbed mental well-being running through the chapters surrounding Sarah's death. When Abraham's servant returns with Isaac's future wife, Rebekah, Isaac is found meditating in a field, seeking peace and respite, we assume from his own distress. When he and Rebekah come together as husband and wife we are told that finally Isaac found comfort following the death of his mother.[160]

The Bible does not shy away from understanding that our well-being is determined as much by our mental state as our physical state. Moses in his earlier life is a man who stutters, a physical trait that often has emotional difficulties as its underlying cause.[161] The prophet Ezekiel lives with wild visions which compel him to speak out in the Babylonian exile.[162] King Saul loses his monarchy to David because his mental illness makes it impossible for him to cope with the role.[163] Hannah, the mother of the prophet Samuel, first appears in the Book of Samuel as a woman in "bitterness of soul, who weeps continuously".[164]

---

[158] Midrash Genesis Rabbah 58:5
[159] Related in Genesis Chapter 22
[160] Genesis 24:63ff
[161] Exodus 4:10
[162] Ezekiel 1:5ff
[163] 1 Samuel 16:14ff
[164] 1 Samuel 1:9

From the story of Abraham we learn the *mitzvah* of *Bikkur Cholim*, the Jewish duty literally to visit the sick. It comes from the point where Abraham is recovering from his circumcision and God appears to him as he sits at the door of his tent.[165] From here our rabbis derive that each of us, too, has a duty to be there for others who are not well, to be involved in each other's illnesses and, hopefully, recovery.[166] This duty does not apply to physical illness only but to mental illness as well. The priest Eli encounters the deeply distressed Hannah. His reaction to her distress is not rejection but compassion and care, and for that reason Hannah decides to dedicate her son Samuel's life to the Temple service and he grows up to be one of the great prophets of Israel.

When Solomon Ibn Gabirol in eleventh-century Spain writes of the greatest Jewish duties, *mitzvot* towards one another, he writes that we must "*v'ha-dalim t'rachem, v'ha'aveilim t'nachem, v'hacholim t'sichem*", a rhyming formulation that dictates compassion for the needy, comfort for the mourners, and conversation (*sichah*) for the sick.

In our community we talk quite freely about and support each other pretty effectively when our physical health is challenged. This has not always been easy. A generation ago it was very difficult to find support and to express freely one's feelings about cancer or living with HIV, for example. Now, through the work of Jewish charities like Chai Cancer Care and JAT and their counterparts in wider society, and through an opening up of our community to the issues, the situation is much better. Relatives and people living with the trauma of physical illness can find action and support rapidly.

This is much less the case with issues around mental well-being. As rabbis we often hear families speaking about how difficult it is to share the challenge of supporting a relative whose mental health is not good, whether for short or long periods. We hear about people finding it

---

[165] Genesis 18:1
[166] Babylonian Talmud Nedarim 39b-40a

difficult to find support from friends and from health services. We hear about people feeling cut off from their various communities.

Mental health is the new frontier of compassion, of *bikkur cholim*. We hear more as each year passes about the challenges to mental health services and the problems that come from taboos around discussing it. We need to make our communities places where, as is already the case with physical illness, you know you can talk about mental well-being with frankness and find support, not ostracism.

Our Torah recognises that our mental well-being is also a matter of concern for people around us. We should never be isolated because our mental health is challenged. We may not live to one-hundred and twenty-seven but our lives are long enough for many ups and downs. We can help each other and our families to survive the downs so that we can enjoy the ups together.

# Who Would Have Thought That Religion Would Still Be A Player?

THEY STARTED AT Lands End with 1400 miles ahead of them. They finished at John O'Groats, sore, soaking wet from the rain but, not surprisingly, elated. This was the Rabbi Relay Ride, a fabulous enterprise led by the Jewish food and environmental charity Gefiltefest in 2012. The idea was that a core team of three extraordinarily fit young people would ride day after day all the way from the foot of Cornwall to the pinnacle of Scotland, joined by others for sections of the route. Each day they would be joined by a rabbi, challenging themselves to cycle the fifty-five miles or more in a day from point to point, raising money by sponsorship for a charity of their choice. The rabbis included Rabbi Harvey Belovski of the Golders Green United Synagogue, Rabbi Anna Gerrard of the Gloucestershire Liberal Jewish Community, Rabbi Jeremy Gordon of the Masorti New London Synagogue and myself.

Each day began the same as the rabbi for the day blew a shofar to start the riders off. On my day we began in Alwoodley, the very Jewish part of Leeds where the sight of a rabbi, assorted kippot and the sound of a shofar is nothing unusual. We cycled across the Yorkshire moors for seven solid hours, in, thank goodness, sunshine and a cooling breeze.

We went through villages where large groups of Jews are rarely if ever seen, stopping for lunch (kosher peanut butter sandwiches) in a village called Kilburn. Seventy-three miles later we crossed the River Tees, having left Yorkshire behind. I left the ride in Yarm, a pretty historic village where I suspect my blow of the shofar may have been the first ever heard. Then I, a Reform rabbi, handed over the shofar to Rabbi Geoffrey Hyman of Ilford United Synagogue, who took it onwards for two gruelling days until the ride reached Edinburgh. I returned to London and cycled my final ten miles from King's Cross to our home.

The Torah from the middle of the Book of Exodus to the end of the Book of Deuteronomy is the story of a journey of forty years. After so many years of wandering in the wilderness, Moses is told that he cannot continue as the leader who will bring the Children of Israel into the Promised Land. Yet still he continues to lead until they reach its very borders, having struggled their way through opposing peoples.

As religion does when it is a great contributor to the world, the vision of achieving the Promised Land drives the Children of Israel and their leader Moses on to a better future. So, too, in a small but still personally challenging way did the riders on the Rabbi Relay Ride, each of us turning the wheels for causes which aim to relieve poverty or distress.

Religion is not a private affair. It is not only a matter between a person and their relationship with God. Religion is rather the guide that helps to mediate our relationships with all humanity and to drive us onwards towards building a better world for this and future generations. As it says in the Psalms, "*sh'viti Adonai l'negdi tamid*, I keep God before me always."[167] Many synagogues and Jewish homes have a plaque saying this on prominent display.

Take religion out of the public sphere, as if you ever could, and humankind has an aimlessness which can lead to the dominance of the bully, the neglect of the disadvantaged and the survival only of the powerful. Religion mandates us to do better than this.

However, religion can, of course, be a cover for some of the worst aspects of humanity. Whatever our scriptures say, whether we be Jew, Christian, Muslim or followers of any faith, we have to put our God-given faculties of choice-making and seeking the moral way that builds the greatest human happiness as an interpretative filter upon our traditions. Rabbi Jonathan Sacks said, "Scripture without commentary is like dynamite without protection."

---

[167] Psalm 16:8

Muslim scholar Mohammed al Hussaini helps us to understand some of the choices that have been made in Islamist doctrine over the past decades. A line of interpretation of the Koran has led to the ideology behind the Muslim Brotherhood and further into the ideology behind Al-Quaeda and Daesh. It is, he says, an ideology of humiliation. The idea is that Islam is at a point where it has been humiliated by Western ideas and ways of living which have taken root in Muslim societies.

Thus the passages in the Koran which preach co-existence and the rights of other peoples to self-determination must, for Islamists, be set aside for the time being until Islam has, in their eyes, a rightful place of dominance. Sheikh Al Hussaini teaches texts from the Koran and their traditional interpretation which assert the right of the Jews to the Land of Israel. These have been set aside by Islamists on the basis, they allege, that Zionism is a western ideology and not truly part of Judaism. It is an Islam which cannot cope with a pluralist world. As we know, at its worst it is very dangerous for the world.

Something of the same takes place in Israel itself, too. Kibbutz Gezer is a beautiful green Kibbutz in the hills near Modi'in. It has a population of around 400 people and is a centre for the local area. Within the Kibbutz is a synagogue called Birkat Shalom, blessing of peace. The Kibbutz was founded in 1945 but has thrived only in the past couple of decades, enough to build a synagogue within its grounds.

In 2006 the community decided that it had grown enough to merit a rabbi to be attached to it, provided and employed as they normally are by the Ministry of Religion in Israel. Four thousand rabbis are employed and deployed to congregations and the army and other institutions by the Israel Ministry of Religion. The thing is, the community of Kibbutz Gezer and the area around is made up mostly of Jews who share the values of Reform Judaism, and so what they wanted was a Reform rabbi, preferably the rabbi who was already working with their community, Miri Gold.

Now the four thousand rabbis at that time employed by the State of Israel are different from Rabbi Miri Gold in two respects: number one, they are all men, and number two, they are all Orthodox. So a campaign began by the people of Kibbutz Gezer, championed by the Israel Religious Action Centre, to ensure that the State of Israel recognises that there is more than one way to be a Jew. Thus, if the state is going to provide rabbis for congregations, there must be more than one kind of rabbi on offer. After seven years of campaigning, the Israeli Attorney General ruled that this was indeed so, and Rabbi Miri Gold became the first Reform rabbi to be granted a state salary on the same basis as Orthodox community rabbis. So far, so excellently good and a great fillip to the thirty congregations of the Israel Movement for Progressive Judaism, who may in the future not be discriminated against because their Judaism is not Orthodox.

However, soon after the ruling was promulgated, the Sephardi Chief Rabbi of Israel, Rabbi Shlomo Amar, announced that he was calling upon his fellow Orthodox rabbis to prevent the implementation of the Attorney General's ruling. He sent a letter to hundreds of Orthodox rabbis in Israel calling on them to object to Rabbi Gold's employment and inviting them to an emergency meeting in Jerusalem.

In his letter, Rabbi Amar lamented, "The hand given to the up rooters and destroyers of Judaism who have already wrought horrible destruction upon the People of Israel in the Diaspora by causing terrible assimilation and the uprooting of all of the Torah's precepts. And now they seek recognition in the Land of Israel as well, to be destroyers of the religion ... This will not pass!" He added, "No one may be absent from the gathering."

Rabbi Amar's letter is not Judaism as a source of vision for our people, rather this is the instigation of, in Anat Hoffman of the Israel Religious Action Centre's words, *sinat hinam,* the kind of senseless hatred that has been at the root of Judaism's disasters over the millennia. She wrote that, "The reality is that most Jews, from all denominations, want Israel to be the physical and spiritual home for the entire Jewish people."

153

Religion should be a source of vision and a positive future, a set of tools that build the world. It should not be a sledgehammer to deal violently with perceived humiliations, as is fundamentalist Islam. It should not be a chainsaw to rip a people apart, as is the denying by the Israel Chief Rabbinate of the right of Jews to express their Judaism in the way that is true to themselves. In the end, it is up to us to interpret the meaning of our religions and the texts which support our religious life in a direction that builds and does not destroy, that supports and does not crush, that cares and does not reject.

As the Rabbi Relay Riders reached John O'Groats they had shown that there is more than one way to be an energetic Jew or even a foolhardy rabbi. May religions always be such a positive force in our lives.

# Jewish Thought

# The Fundamental Truth Is A Lie

AS A HAPPY and settled Progressive rabbi there was one rabbinic job advertisement in the *Jewish Chronicle* newspaper a few years ago which was for a little while rather tempting, if only for the mischief that I could cause by applying. This was the advertisement for a Chief Rabbi of the United Kingdom and Commonwealth, to take the place of Rabbi Lord Jonathan Sacks.

Now I am not suggesting that I could perform such a role with any distinction, but there was something missing from the advert which gave me an opening. Nowhere in the advert did it specify that the applicant needed to be an Orthodox rabbi. It would have been fun to see what would have happened if I, a Progressive rabbi by upbringing and a Reform rabbi by conviction, sent in an application. Now of course I didn't, but I should have been warned off even contemplating it by what happened to the Chief Rabbi of Lemberg, now called Lvov, in Poland, a city with a Jewish population in the nineteenth and early twentieth centuries of more than 150,000 Jews.

Rabbi Avraham Kohn was appointed Chief Rabbi of Lemberg in 1844. He was an enlightened intellectual who had studied at the University of Prague and had been ordained into the fast-growing Reform rabbinate. He was also an excellent community organiser and, in his new post, served the Jews of Lemberg well by establishing a secondary school where secular subjects were taught to a high standard alongside Judaism, establishing a major Reform synagogue in the city, and successfully campaigning for the removal of an unjust tax imposed by the city on Shabbat candles and kosher meat.

Somebody did not like what he was doing. On 6th September 1848, Abraham Ber Pilpel entered the kitchen of Rabbi Abraham Kohn's apartment and poured arsenic in the soup that was being prepared for his family's dinner. Within hours, the forty-one-year-old rabbi and his infant daughter were dead. It was never absolutely clear who had hired Abraham Ber Pilpel to murder the reforming Chief Rabbi of Lemberg, but there were many whispers that the people behind the plot were Lemberg's Orthodox leaders who were known to have creamed off much of the Shabbat candle and kosher meat tax. Perhaps he had been hired by people who just objected to Rabbi Kohn's Jewish reforms. We will never know. Rabbi Kohn became Judaism's first and hopefully last martyr to toleration.

In twenty-first-century society there is no such person as a stranger. Where Jews live today, the stranger is your neighbour, and as the central verse of the Torah says, "You must love your neighbour as yourself". When you leave any synagogue in London and walk for a few hundred metres you are bound to encounter people whose family origins span three, perhaps four continents, whose religious traditions include Hinduism, Christianity and Islam as well as several varieties of Judaism. As well as in the Diaspora communities where Jews live, this is increasingly the case in Israel. The material success of our Jewish state means that not only is it home to more than a million Muslim and Christian Arabs but also to many thousands of non-Jewish economic and refugee migrants from Asia and Africa.

Judaism is hard-wired for toleration. We do not see ourselves as the sole possessors of absolute truth. We understand that for a Christian, a Hindu or a Muslim their truth is their way to God. So, by the way, in his heart of hearts did Chief Rabbi Sacks in his book *The Dignity of Difference*, until the more fundamentalist dayanim, who can't accept the relativisation of truth, ensured he republished the book without the tolerant sections.

Moses Mendelssohn, the eighteenth-century German Jewish philosopher who was one of the strongest advocates for Judaism's engagement with the enlightenment, put this elegantly in 1769: "All our rabbis teach unanimously that the written and oral laws in which our revealed religion consists are binding only on our nation. Moses commanded the law for us, it is a legacy of the community of Jacob. All the other peoples of the Earth, we believe, have been instructed by God to observe the law of nature and the religion of the patriarchs [Mendelssohn notes: 'The seven main commandments of the Noachides']. Those who direct their way of life in accordance with this religion of nature and reason are called by other nations virtuous men, and these are children of the eternal blessedness."

The Noachide laws are an early Rabbinic interpretation of the end of the story of Noah which say that as long as a person observes seven basic principles of decency and humanity, such as not killing, having a system of justice and not being excessively cruel to animals, then whatever their religious tradition or beliefs they are just as much to be considered righteous and entitled to a place in the World to Come as any good Jew.[168]

When you walk through the front door of JCoSS, the first pluralist, and therefore tolerant by charter Jewish secondary school in Britain, high up on the wall are these words from the Talmud, "*Eilu v'Eilu Divrei Elohim Chayyim*, Both these and these are the words of the Living God."[169]

The context of *Eilu v'Eilu* is this: "R. Abba stated in the name of Samuel: For three years there was a dispute between Beit Shammai and Beit Hillel, the former asserting, 'The halachah is in agreement with our views' and the latter contending, 'The halachah is in agreement with our views.' Then a *bat kol* was heard announcing, '[The utterances of] both are the words of the living God, but the halachah is in agreement with the rulings of Beit Hillel.' Since, however, 'both are the word of the living God,' what was it that entitled Beth Hillel to have the halachah fixed in agreement with their rulings? Because they were kindly and modest, they studied their own rulings and those of Beit Shammai, and were even so [humble] as to mention the actions of Beit Shammai before their own."

---

[168] Derived from Genesis 9:4-6 and enumerated in Sanhedrin 56a
[169] Babylonian Talmud, Eruvin 13b

Way back in first-century Judaism truth was not absolute but rather there were and are multiple truths and one does not need to squash out the truths of others for your truth to be real.

The way it works is this. All Jews learn authoritatively and authentically from the same texts. We all stood at Sinai together to hear the foundation text, Torah. But where we go from there, how we interpret what Torah means for us today, here and now, diverges and is meant to diverge, for "these and these are the words of the Living God."

It means for a Reform Jew you do find truth. For us, for example, the truth is that men and women are to be equal in Jewish religious duties and observances. For us, the truth is that we are to find our own way of resting and observing God's gift of Shabbat, meaningful to our day. For an Orthodox Jew you find your truth, that men and women should observe separate religious observances, that there is a precise system of what it means to rest on Shabbat. Both are authentic Jewish ways to God. The only thing that isn't is the Jew, or the Christian or the Muslim or the Hindu, who says, "Only my way is the truth – the rest of you are wrong and not to be tolerated."

It is tempting in an uncertain, rapidly changing world, where we seven billion have to share limited space and resources, where the stranger is our neighbour, to seek the certainty that an authority figure can give us. Fundamentalism in its many religious guises dangerously answers this search. It helps people to feel that they are strong in what they think and do.

Really, though, fundamentalism is a weakness that takes you further and further from God. Fundamentalists of any religion make one single image of the God who is all and everywhere, a breach of the Second Commandment.[170] At the root of an authentic search for God is the ability to see truth in all of its multi-coloured, multivalent and diverse

---

[170] Exodus 20:4

glory. Then find your path, joining with others, whilst respecting those who choose differently. I would not have made a good Orthodox Chief Rabbi!

# Who Has Kept Judaism Going All These Years?

IF YOU WERE to meet a Russian in the Old Bull and Bush pub on the hill leading up to Hampstead nowadays, it is quite possible that he or she would be serving behind the bar, as many Russians have immigrated to Britain in the past few years. Thirty years ago, though, it was an altogether more remarkable occurrence. It was in the Old Bull and Bush in 1988 that I first met Andre Kogan. Although he did not know it at the time, Andre was soon to become the first student rabbi from Russia to study at Leo Baeck College in London. He was not able to complete the course, but he blazed a trail that is now followed by at least one or two students in each year at the college.

Andre was in London because, at the World Union for Progressive Judaism Conference in that year, his father Zinovy Kogan had stood up to say *Hineni*, Here I am, the name of the very first Progressive Jewish congregation to be formed in what was still then the USSR. Andre was in London to find out how we run young adult provision in the UK. This was still the time of *refusniks* and restriction of religious freedom in the Soviet Union but the era of *glasnost* and *perestroika* meant that the time was coming for religious freedom to return to Russia. For me, it was extremely exciting to meet Andre and to see that something new was about to begin in the Jewish world, signalled by his very presence in Britain.

Nowadays, there are many Reform Jewish communities in Russia served by rabbis trained at Leo Baeck College, Geiger College and Hebrew Union College. This is such a developed community now that rather than one individual amazing everyone by turning up at a World Union for Progressive Judaism conference, the conference of the 1.5 million Progressive Jews of the world itself took place in Moscow in July 2005.

Very impressive? No? Well not if you count Jewish achievement by numbers. The biggest force in Russian Judaism today is not Progressive Judaism but rather it is Chabad, the Lubavitch. Lubavitch Judaism is available in fifty-five cities in Russia, serviced by not just ten or so Rabbis of Progressive Judaism but 150 Shlichim, most of whom have gained semichah as rabbis, and their wives. Now that's impressive. Surely only the Lubavitch are really able to make Russian Jews be Jews, because of the resources that they have at their disposal? In fact, because of their strength on the Russian scene there is effectively no other Orthodox Jewish presence nor Masorti or Conservative presence in Russia, only Reform Judaism or Lubavitch.

The Lubavitch really are amazing. According to recent estimates published a couple of years ago in Sue Fishkoff's book, *The Rebbe's Army* there are around 100–200,000 members of the Lubavitch Chassidic sect worldwide. From this group, less than a tenth of the number of Progressive Jews, Lubavitch has become effectively a global Jewish brand. There are Chabad houses, Lubavitch Centres, in all of those Russian cities, and from Kathmandu to Brussels, from Tel Aviv to Buenos Aires. At Chanukkah the Lubavitch foundation "Tzivos HaShem" provides the thirty-foot-tall Chanukkiah outside Golders Green Station in London, and Chanukkiot in hundreds of other locations worldwide, literally from Chang Mai in Thailand to Punta Del Este in Uruguay.[171]

Chabad stands for *chochmah* – wisdom, *binah* – understanding and *da'at* – knowledge – and that is what the Lubavitch movement feels that it is spreading throughout the world. To lead those Chabad Houses there are 3,700 Shlichim couples worldwide, perhaps 8,000 people who have dedicated their lives to spreading Judaism the Lubavitch way. It is reckoned that there must be a further 40,000 or so people employed by the Lubavitch worldwide to staff these Chabad houses.

---

[171] Sue Fishkoff, *The Rebbe's Army* (New York: Schoken Books, 2005)

How much does all this cost? Sue Fishkoff estimates that Lubavitch worldwide must have to raise upwards of $250 million-worth of funds each year. Who is providing this level of resources? It seems abundantly clear that a great proportion of this $250 million is coming not from Lubavitch members but from Jews in other movements, mainstream Orthodox, Conservative, Liberal and, who knows, maybe even Reform.

Why are they doing it? Why finance Lubavitch and not their own movements to do the undeniably worthwhile outreach work that Lubavitch does? The reason is, I suspect, because an awful lot of Jews, whatever their own Judaism, persist in the belief that when all is said and done it is ultra-orthodox Judaism that keeps us going as a religion and possibly always has. Never mind the place of women in ultra-orthodoxy, never mind the lack of willingness to engage with modern knowledge, never mind the dynastic nature of leadership, never mind the lack of tolerance of other points of view, never mind the hankering after a personal Messiah, in the case of the Lubavitch, possibly in the person of the last Rebbe, never mind the idea that Jews have a special soul that is not given to other people – never mind everything that makes **us** choose not to be ultra-orthodox Jews, it is they who have enabled Judaism to survive and if they are not strengthened by our donations then Judaism has a limited future.

Really? It's not the way I think! What would happen if the Jewish world was entirely Progressive, by which I mean Reform and Liberal? What would happen if we did not fund ultra-Orthodox Judaism and instead put all our energy into our own form of Judaism? What would happen if the entire Jewish world was inclusive of people who want to find their way into Judaism, accepted that women have a right to an equal role in Judaism and Jewish practice, had to be fully engaged with the world as it is, not separated from it, encouraged inter-faith dialogue, was more interested in the needs of the individual than the face-value demands of Jewish law, worked towards a Messianic Age of peace and unity? Would Judaism die out within a generation or two? Of course not!

But Judaism would have been so vastly changed that I do think we would have lost a great part of what does enable us to survive. That is the bi-polar nature of Judaism. Perhaps it began when many of the exiled Jews in Babylonia decided not to come back to Israel when the opportunity presented itself, thus beginning what Leo Baeck in his seminal work, *The Essence of Judaism*, was to identify as the two creative centres of Judaism, Israel and the Diaspora.[172] Judaism exists, survives and thrives along a spectrum, not as one dogmatic set of beliefs and values. You need the fullness of that spectrum to be available for Judaism to continue to make its contribution to the world.

Judaism exists on a spectrum, which, it could be said, imitates the qualities of the Holy One. This spectrum runs from *din* (law and its strict application) to *rachmanut* (compassion). Often these attributes are contrasted as "justice" and "mercy". In many synagogues what really matters is that the law is adhered to – for these synagogues it is Jewish law and its strict application that binds the Jewish community together, and if that excludes children from learning about their heritage because the "wrong" parent is Jewish, or if that excludes someone whose sexual orientation is not covered by that law from being part of the community, or if that tends to divide Jews from people of other religions living in the same area, then so be it.

In a Reform synagogue, what really matters is that we are compassionate, for in Reform synagogues it is our compassion for our fellow Jews and for humanity in general that binds the Jewish community together. When that compassion enables a family where one partner is Jewish and the other is not to be active in Jewish life and to bring their children up as Jews, when that enables a gay couple to bring the best in themselves to Judaism, and when that enables us to create friendly relationships with people of all faiths, people in a Reform synagogue are delighted.

---

[172] Leo Beack, *The Essence of Judaism* (New York: Schoken Books, 1948)

But that is not to say that in the law-dominated synagogues there is no care for people or that in our compassion-dominated synagogues there are no standards. Far from it. Jewish law encourages each Jew to care deeply about each other - to visit the sick, comfort the bereaved and much more. Similarly, because a Reform synagogue is a compassionate community, we have developed standards and rituals from the wellspring of Jewish tradition, so that we are able to be clear about which obligations and responsibilities being Jewish places upon us.

Because Reform Judaism is a movement where compassion is one of our guiding principles, and in our synagogues men and women are equal participants in all aspects of Jewish life, we encourage a wide-ranging debate about our Jewish State of Israel, where we care about all of the peoples who live in and around the Land, not only the Jews. In our Progressive synagogues we provide Jewish learning for all ages, where there is no such thing as a silly question and our rabbis are, we hope, particularly approachable and do not take the role of sitting in judgement on the lives of our members, but rather see themselves as focussed on helping each person to continue on their Jewish journey.

Reform Judaism is the innovative force in Judaism which challenges those to the right of us to find their way to respond to the needs of people. Meanwhile, Orthodox Judaism challenges us Reform Jews to respond creatively to the tradition which it conserves. We need each other to survive. Reaching back into the lessons of history from Babylonia and Israel, to Hillel and Shammai, to Ashkenazi and Sephardi, polar diversity in Judaism has always strengthened, not weakened us.

The Progressive tendency in Judaism has enabled us to survive forces that would have destroyed us had we been rigid. Jochanon ben Zakkai remoulded Jewish practice outside the Temple when Jerusalem was lost. Hillel voided the requirements of Jewish financial law when he saw that it was causing Jews to fail to support the needy. Maimonides developed our theology to respond to the intellectual attractiveness of Islam. The early Jewish reformers built a Jewish response to the enlightenment and emancipation. And so we are still here, a thriving community worldwide and in Israel, contributing to the world well beyond our numbers. The light of the *Ner Tamid* continues to burn, fuelled by the diversity within Judaism. The oil our opponents thought would burn out in a day has lasted eight-fold. With our help and dedication, the Reform contribution to that light will remain strong for the Jews of the former Soviet Union as much as for ourselves.

# The Fruitless Search For An Easy Life

I AM RATHER proud of our Sukkah at our synagogue. It's properly covered with laurel grown right here on the synagogue site. Look carefully and you will see it includes synagogue members' rhubarb stalks, vines, a passion flower plant, flowers grown in members' gardens, streamers made out of recycled plastic bags, discarded computer mice gaining new life masquerading as fruit and all of the flowers which enhanced our services on Rosh Hashanah and Yom Kippur enjoying a second life as part of the Sukkah. What may not be obvious is how all of this got there, especially the laurel right on the top of the large Sukkah.

Something special is needed every year. We need the Israeli men to turn up to help build the Sukkah. What I mean by this is that there are many kinds of fellow among the synagogue membership, but most being regular Jewish men like myself, none of us, with just a couple of well-known exceptions, are much good at anything resembling DIY. And building a Sukkah certainly does resemble DIY.

Our synagogue's Israeli male members are not quite the same. They can do DIY. They spent two years in the army learning to maintain tanks and all kinds of things. In Israel there is no-one else to send out for to do the DIY, so Israeli men have to be able to do it.

What that means for our Sukkah is that whilst we Diaspora men carefully and gingerly climb ladders to put bits of laurel on the top, two Israeli men pull themselves up onto the very top of the structure of the Sukkah. They straddle it and get the children below to throw them up the *shchah*, the covering for the Sukkah, so that our laurel gets into places few Diaspora men could manage!

Our Sukkah, as a result, does a great job of celebrating the bounty of how we benefit from the harvests which bring us our food. As we are told in the Torah reading which begins Sukkot, "When you have gathered in your harvest then celebrate, enjoy a festival."[173] The reading includes the command to dwell in Sukkahs so that you will always remember that you were liberated from Egypt and struggled through the desert living in simple shelters.[174]

Why ruin a nice celebration of delight with memories of a struggle? What is going on? The Torah seems to be full of these conundrums. Things seem to be going well, but then it all goes wrong.

Adam and Eve are in paradise in the Garden of Eden, then they eat the fruit which they are forbidden and they are expelled from the Garden.[175] Abraham and Sarah have their longed-for child Isaac, then Abraham is asked to offer him up as a sacrifice.[176] Jacob is settled in the land of his wanderings and then his daughter Dinah is taken off by a local chieftain.[177] The Israelites are living well in Goshen in Egypt, then the new Pharaoh becomes scared of them and enslaves them.[178] They are freed from slavery, then find their way blocked by the Sea of Reeds.[179] When the Israelites are in the desert and wandering towards their Promised Land, the water runs out.[180] They are ready to enter the Promised Land and then have to join in battle against the Moabites.[181]

It is as if the life of our people is a continual series of struggles and obstacles to be overcome. It is as if being connected to God by covenant and being part of a religion and a religious people does not grant you an easy life, but rather brings you into a constant series of *tsourises*.

---

[173] Leviticus 23:39
[174] Leviticus 23:42-43
[175] Genesis 3:23-24
[176] Genesis 22:1-2
[177] Genesis Chapter 34
[178] Exodus Chapter 1
[179] Exodus Chapter 14
[180] Numbers Chapter 20
[181] Numbers Chapter 21

Of course, it's actually the other way round. Life, real life, is normally, unless you are exceptionally lucky, punctuated or even beset with a constant series of struggles and challenges. Life does not run easily. Religious life does not grant you a pass through these struggles. Bad things do happen to good people.

The story of the Jewish people emphasises this trajectory. Reflecting the struggles in the Torah, the history of the Jewish people records times of peace and progress punctuated by terrible challenges and disaster, from the Hadrianic persecutions to the Crusades to the mass expulsions of Jewish communities throughout Europe, to the mass murder of the Shoah. Even now we have Israel, the Jewish State is constantly beset with challenges to its very existence.

You can see the effect of our troubled history in every Jewish wedding ceremony. Jewish weddings used to be two-part ceremonies, a betrothal, called *Erusin,* followed by the wedding itself, up to a year later, called *Nissuin.* Because it became too uncertain in too many places that the couple would still be able to travel to each other, or even that both bride and groom would still be traceable, in the twelfth century the two ceremonies were combined into one as we now have it. The natural world and our own bodies are too fragile, the human scene too volatile, relationships too diverse and interactive for a smooth path through life to be possible for anyone.

So what is Judaism for, then, if it is not to give us a pass to a straightforward life? It is not and it never was. Rather, what it means to be a Jew is to be granted the opportunity to find support and care throughout the inevitable struggles of life. It means that you will be part of a community which will, if it follows the principles of our religion's requirements for relationships between people, give you support and care, whether or not you are family. It means that you will feel God's guiding hand giving shape and meaning to your life. It will bring you into relationship with millions of others who share your struggles through the world, who will take you in and feed you when you need

169

them. Through the festivals it will give you opportunities to celebrate, to find joy in the best way we can, with others of all generations.

Judaism recognises that life is a struggle, personally, communally and existentially, a point made clearly in the Megillah for Sukkot, Kohelet, which argues that in the end all is vanity.[182] So what we need and what true Judaism provides is a way of making it through the tough times and creating many good times. For me it is one of the many things I love about our religion. It's not here to say the world should be easy for good people. Rather, it's here to help me find a way through good and bad and to move me to try to bring better for the world around me. Taking this back to Israel for a moment, the Jewish State does not live easily, of course. Its young men and women are trained to deal with the struggle and to find their way round tough times that have been in the past and might yet come again. Maybe that is why our synagogue's Israeli members climbed up onto the top of our Sukkah to make sure that our celebration was complete! They have wandered through the desert and will go to any lengths to give us shade.

---

[182] Ecclesiastes Chapter 1ff

# Will The Real Monotheist Please Stand Up?

I HAVE ONLY ever met one Druid priestess. I was in Manchester recording a programme in the always stimulating "Beyond Belief" series on BBC Radio 4. This series, hosted by Ernie Rae, provides an island of high quality religious discussion amongst the week's output of secular life.

The reason why I was there with the Druid priestess, Emma Restall Orr, was that the subject that they wanted to discuss is the contrast between polytheism, the belief in many Gods, and monotheism, the belief that there is but one God. The "Beyond Belief" producer reckoned that she would get pretty good value out of a discussion between a Druid who understands the world to be at one with gods from the Greek tradition, ancient Anglo-Saxon traditions and rather special things about trees, and a rabbi from the Jewish tradition who is therefore under the obligation to say, "Hear O Israel the Eternal One is our God, the Eternal God is One", twice a day, every day, but who, being a Progressive Jew, would at least be able to engage in meaningful discussion with a person whose views would seem to be diametrically opposed to his. Indeed, our discussion was, I felt, most meaningful and interesting. Our Druid priestess was not quite as clearly polytheistic as you might think. The basis of Druidism, as she explained it, being that one understands the whole of the world and universe, yourself included, to be one organic whole, the gods, in her understanding, being concentrations of energy within that whole. It's almost monotheism.

The prophet Isaiah was a passionate opponent of polytheism. Much of his message is one of severe criticism of the Israelites for having tried to hedge their bets over the intervening years between the days of Moses and his own by worshipping the local land gods, fertility gods, harvest and weather gods of the peoples among whom they lived, alongside the Jewish God. The Israelites were living as if Adonai was merely one of a series of forces that needed to be called upon to their benefit, rather than the single force guaranteeing their ethics, promising redemption and having brought them to be as a people.

I had a potentially very embarrassing experience with Isaiah a while ago, when the father of a child who was about to experience baby naming and introduction into the Jewish community read a Haftarah from the beginning of the words of the Second Isaiah.[183] The baby-naming ceremony was wonderfully life-affirming for our Judaism as the mother of the child was not born Jewish, but the couple had been clear, from when they got together, that they would bring up any children they might have as Jews. Here it was beginning to happen as their first son was named in synagogue. They were, thank goodness, members of a synagogue open to accept them and enable Judaism to live on in their generation, the couple standing proudly together and grandparents of both sides there in synagogue with them. There was a problem, though, because the Isaiah passage for the week was one which condemns idols and the worship of other gods in strong language. As the father of the baby stepped up to read the Haftarah the insensitivity hit me, his wife is of Hindu heritage and her parents are practising Hindus, her father clearly so, from the *bindi* on his forehead, demonstrating recent devotions. How would they feel hearing this, worshipping a multiplicity of gods and statues representing them being crucial to Hindu practice. They would not know that we hadn't picked the Haftarah specifically as a way of making them feel unwelcome in the synagogue.

In the event, the mother's Hindu parents and their son-in-law had in fact discussed the portion before the reading and had come to understand why it was the one assigned for that Shabbat, but more importantly they did not see it as being applied to them as Hindus. The Hindu grandparents understand their religion to be monotheistic but that the gods in their house are merely representations of ways of relating to the One God. This I found out speaking to the family straight after the service.

---

[183] Isaiah Chapter 40

Should we, though, as an inclusive synagogue, have chosen not to use the traditional Haftarah portion in sensitivity to the presumed feelings of the Hindu grandparents of this Jewish child, and of course to his mother's heritage?

The Orthodox Chief Rabbi Jonathan Sacks was in no doubt what he should do when faced with the possibility of being near to something that current strict Halachic opinion considers idolatry, the statuary and iconography of a Catholic cathedral. So it was at the funeral of Cardinal Basil Hume in Westminster Cathedral in 1999 that Rabbi Sacks kept a discreet but definite distance from the event by watching it on a television screen in the cathedral precincts rather than being in the body of the cathedral. When I was discussing this event with Ernie Rea before we recorded the programme, he remarked that in his past life as a young Presbyterian minister in Northern Ireland he had been censured by the elders of his church for visiting the local Catholic church for the installation of a new priest. He was seen by them to be consorting with idolaters. But of course, if you ask a Catholic if they are a monotheist, if they believe in one God, they will say "yes", and so no Progressive rabbi would feel that they should not attend an event in a Catholic church out of principle.

So if a Druid priestess, a Hindu devotee and a Catholic Christian are all monotheists, what does it mean when a Bar or Bat Mitzvah child in our synagogue steps forward holding the Torah the moment before they read from it and says loud and proud, "*Shema Yisrael Adonai Eloheynu Adonai Echad*"? What if anything is distinctly Jewish about our assertions about the one God?

For an answer to this you need to do a very Reform Jewish thing and look back into the history of the development of our relationship with and understanding of God. Our spiritual ancestors were undoubtedly worshippers in the traditions of the people amongst whom they lived, as we say each year in our Seder service. These traditions included the worship of their ancestors, stories of the creation of the world which involve the capriciousness of warring gods, and the worship of the phenomena of nature. You can identify vestigial signs of these beliefs in the Psalms and elsewhere in the Bible. But at some point they came to believe that one particular understanding of God was the way to know the deity of their tribe, El, or El Shaddai, which we nowadays translate as "the Almighty".[184]

This was the God of Abraham, Isaac and Jacob, personal, relational, strong and worth arguing and bargaining with. However you may feel about the historical veracity of the actual narrative in the Torah, there can be no doubt that it represents a stage in our development when the ancestors of Jews were not yet monotheistic. Rather they were monolatrous, worshipping and feeling themselves under the influence of, and in a covenantal relationship with one God only, but able to accept the existence and reality of the many other god figures that were equally central to the people around them, Baal of the Canaanites, Marduk of the Babylonians, Dagan the harvest god, etc.

This monolatrous understanding of the Divine continues into the Moses narrative, where our God shows that He is stronger and more effective than the god of the Egyptians, Pharaoh. The early story of the Exodus is a battle presented as a war of the gods over nature, the plagues, in which Pharaoh is hopelessly outclassed by Elohim, our God. In a historical reading of Torah our God is not the only divine being understood to exist, rather He is simply the best. The Shema in the Torah means not that God is one but that God is alone in what He does and, as Moses explicitly says in his last song, "No alien god was with Him"[185] and, as he sings as the Children of Israel cross the Red Sea, "Who is like You among the gods men worship?"[186]

Jews became true monotheists sometime between the time of the Prophets, much of whose message is lambasting us for not being so, and

---

[184] See Exodus 6:3 and Genesis 17:1
[185] Deuteronomy 32:12
[186] Exodus 15:11

the Rabbinic period of Mishnah and Talmud. This means that we came to recognise that the moral and ethical code which we hear from the Torah cannot have eternal value, cannot be a universal system for us to try to make the world a good place if there is room in it for the existence of other divine forces. These divine forces might be other gods or the existence of separate divine forces of good and evil in the doctrine which developed in Gnosticism that became Zoroastrianism. Rather, since we feel that our God demands that we be just, compassionate stewards of the Earth, God must effectively be the God of all. It is just that we Jews relate to God's will though the *mitzvot* that we perform and the laws that we have derived from our understanding of what God needs us to do to repair His world. So, for Jews, monotheism is not only about the number of gods but also about the nature of God.

When we say *Shema Yisrael* we are not just counting God and reaching one. We are saying that the one God needs us to be fully in relationship with Him, active partners in making a better world and repairing what people have broken in the justice due the world. Jewish monotheism combines the understanding of the unity of the world, which many religions share, with the knowledge that we have the responsibility to act as if we are God's hands, to provide the force and power for good.

# INDEX

| | | | |
|---|---|---|---|
| Abraham | 8,56,66,76,79,102, | Heschel, Rabbi | 103-105 |
| | 141,146-148, | Abraham Joshua | |
| | 169,174 | Heschel, Susannah | 106 |
| Abuse of power | 15-18 | Hillel | 32,158,165 |
| Al Hussaini, | 152 | Hitchhiker's Guide to | 40 |
| Mohammed | | the Galaxy | |
| Amar, Rabbi Shlomo | 153 | Hoffman, Anat | 102,153 |
| Anthropocene Era | 55-57 | Hoffman, Rabbi | 117 |
| Balaam | 2,8-9 | Lawrence | |
| Bar & Bat Mitzvah | 30,40,110, | Holocene Era | 55 |
| | 115-119,173 | Ibn Gabirol, Solomon | 148 |
| Bayfield, Rabbi Tony | 22 | Investment | 26-28 |
| Ben-Gurion, David | 85 | Jonas, Rabbi Regina | 106,140 |
| Bikkur Cholim | 148-149 | Josephus, Flavius | 130 |
| Birkat HaMazon | 65,92,111-112 | Karaites | 121 |
| Borowitz, Rabbi | 37 | Kashrut | 5,45, |
| Eugene | | | 95-100,176 |
| Burden, Rabbi Janet | 61 | Ketubot | 124-127 |
| Cain | 42-43,50 | Kohn, Rabbi | 156-157 |
| Cave of Machpelah | 102-103 | Avraham | |
| Chabad – Lubavitch | 82,162-163,176 | Kotel (Western Wall) | 101-102,104 |
| Chad Gadya | 17,107 | Laban | 9 |
| Chief Rabbinate | 153-157,160,173 | Language of prayer | 81-82 |
| Cyprus | 84-85,87-88 | Last words | 4,11-13 |
| Dayenu | 67,107-109 | Leo Baeck College | 102,115, |
| Diamant, Anita | 124 | | 136-137, |
| Economic life | 129 | | 140-143,161 |
| Elijah | 12,65-69,87, | London | 2-3,157 |
| | 89-93,95 | Luria, Rabbi Isaac | 37-38 |
| Engleman, Rabbi | 13 | Maimonides | 22,51,82,96,165 |
| Joshua | | Martyrdom | 29,30-31,157 |
| Exodus refugee vessel | 35-36 | Mendelssohn, Moses | 157-158 |
| Fair trade | 9,59,61-63,99 | Mental health | 147-149 |
| Fundamentalism | 159 | Micro-finance | 52-53 |
| Gold, Rabbi Miri | 152-153 | Monotheism | 7-9,171-175 |
| Haggadah | 17,66-67,86, | Montagu, Lily | 139 |
| | 108-109 | | |

| | | | |
|---|---|---|---|
| Moses | 66,68,70,74, 76-78,120,125, 128,139,143,146 151,158,171,174 | Schwartzman, Rabbi Amy | 59-60,177 |
| Narrative | 18,48,77,85-86 | Seder meal | 17,65-68,77,83, 87,92,106 |
| Ner Tamid | 132-134,166 | Shabbat | 4,9,27-29, 103-105,113, 119-122,129, 131,159 |
| Pardes Institute | 7 | | |
| Pesach | 66,68,85-86,89, 91,95-96,98,106 | | |
| | | Shabbat HaGadol | 66,91,95 |
| Pinker, Steven | 19 | Shammai | 158,165 |
| Pittsburgh Platform | 98 | Shema | 20-21,56,81-82, 173-175 |
| Poverty | 23,26-27,51,60, 62,151 | | |
| | | Shweiger, Rabbi Meir | 7 |
| Rabbinate | 78,110,136-137, 141,143-144 | St Louis refugee vessel | 35 |
| Rabbi Relay Ride | 150,154 | Spectrum of Judaism | 164 |
| Rashi | 73 | Spiro, Nitza | 79-80 |
| Rayner, Rabbi John | 65,82,141 | Stewardship of the Earth | 26,57 |
| Reform Judaism | 52,72-74,77-78, 83,87,98-99, 116-117,122,124, 152,156,159, 163-165,173 | | |
| | | Sukkot | 44-48,86, 168,170 |
| | | Tabick, Rabbi Jackie | 136-138 |
| | | Technology | 51,53,104 119-120,122 |
| Religion | 20,26,78, 112-113,126,144, 150-151,154,158, 168,170 | | |
| | | Tikkun Olam | 38 |
| | | Tzedakah | 51,101 |
| | | Tdedek UK | 51 |
| Romain, Rabbi Jonathan | 32 | Weddings | 110-111, 124-125,169 |
| Rosten, Leo | 79 | Wilderness | 35-36,90-91, 108,128-131 |
| Sabbatical year, Shmittah | 103,130-131 | | |
| | | Women rabbis | 59-60,106, 136-140,163 |
| Sacks, Rabbi Jonathan | 67-68,86,151, 156-157,173 | | |
| | | World Union for Progressive Judaism | 161 |
| Salkin, Rabbi Jeffery | 115 | | |
| Samaritans | 121 | Yoffie, Rabbi Eric | 87 |
| Sarah | 56,102,146-147, 168 | Yom HaShoah | 68 |
| | | Yom HaZikaron | 68-69 |
| Shachter-Shalomi, Rabbi Zalman | 99 | | |

## INDEX OF BIBLICAL AND RABBINIC TEXT REFERENCES

# Torah

| Bereshit (Name of Sedra) | | | |
|---|---|---|---|
| Genesis 1:1 | 11 | | |
| Genesis 1:31 | 41 | | |
| Genesis 2:3 | 104 | | |
| Genesis 2:9 | 56 | | |
| Genesis 3:23 | 72,168 | | |
| Genesis 4:9 | 42,43,50 | | |
| Genesis 5:27 | 146 | | |
| *Noach* | | | |
| Genesis 9:4 | 96 | | |
| Genesis 9:4-6 | 158 | | |
| *Lech Lecha* | | | |
| Genesis 13:13 | 14 | | |
| Genesis 17:1 | 174 | | |
| *Vayeira* | | | |
| Genesis 18:1 | 148 | | |
| Genesis 18:20 | 8 | | |
| Genesis 22 | 147 | | |
| Genesis 22:1-2 | 168 | | |
| Genesis 22:3 | 8 | | |
| *Chayei Sarah* | | | |
| Genesis 23 | 102 | | |
| Genesis 23:1 | 146 | | |
| Genesis 24:20 | 142 | | |
| Genesis 24:63 | 147 | | |
| *Vayeitzei* | | | |
| Genesis 30:27 | 9 | | |
| Genesis 31:49 | 9 | | |
| *Vayishlach* | | | |
| Genesis 34 | 72 | | |
| *Vayechi* | | | |
| Genesis 47:20 | 13 | | |
| *Shemot* | | | |
| Exodus 1 | 168 | | |
| Exodus 3:2 | 129 | | |
| Exodus 4:10 | 147 | | |

| *Va'eira* | | |
|---|---|---|
| Exodus 6:3 | 174 | |
| Exodus 6:6-8 | 67 | |
| *Bo* | | |
| Exodus 10:9 | 139,140 | |
| *Beshelach* | | |
| Exodus 14 | 168 | |
| Exodus 15:11 | 15,174 | |
| Exodus 16 | 106 | |
| *Yitro* | | |
| Exodus 19:2 | 128 | |
| Exodus 20:4 | 159 | |
| Exodus 20:7 | 8 | |
| *Mishpatim* | | |
| Exodus 21:1-6 | 8,16 | |
| Exodus 22:25-26 | 16 | |
| Exodus 23:2,3,6 | 16,17 | |
| Exodus 23:19 | 97 | |
| *Terumah* | | |
| Exodus 25:8 | 134 | |
| *Tetzaveh* | | |
| Exodus 27:20 | 133 | |
| *Vayakhel* | | |
| Exodus 35:2 | 121 | |
| *Shemini* | | |
| Leviticus 11:45 | 96,100 | |
| *Tazria-Metzora* | | |
| Leviticus 12-15 | 72 | |
| *Kedoshim* | | |
| Leviticus 19 | 72 | |
| Leviticus 19:9-10 | 12 | |
| Leviticus 19:13 | 5,16 | |
| Leviticus 19:15 | 16 | |
| Leviticus 19:17 | 61 | |
| *Emor* | | |
| Leviticus 22:32 | 29 | |
| Leviticus 23-25 | 129 | |

| | |
|---|---|
| Leviticus 23:3 | 27 |
| Leviticus 23:39 | 46,168 |
| Leviticus 23:42-43 | 168 |
| Leviticus 24:2 | 133 |
| *Behar* | |
| Leviticus 25:1-24 | 12 |
| Leviticus 25:14 | 62 |
| *Bechukkotai* | |
| Leviticus 26:3-46 | 126 |
| *Bamidbar* | |
| Numbers 1:20 | 38 |
| Numbers 2-4 | 131 |
| *Naso* | |
| Numbers 6:24 | 6 |
| Numbers 6:26 | 21 |
| Numbers 7:9 | 71 |
| *Beha'alotcha* | |
| Numbers 11 | 106 |
| Numbers 11:5-6 | 109 |
| *Chukkat* | |
| Numbers 20 | 70,168 |
| Numbers 21 | 168 |
| Numbers 22:8 | 8 |
| Numbers 22:22 | 8 |
| Numbers 24:5 | 2 |
| *Ekev* | |
| Deuteronomy 8:5 | 114 |
| Deuteronomy 8:10 | 112 |
| Deuteronomy 9:1 | 21,117 |
| *Re'eh* | |
| Deuteronomy 11:13 | 56 |
| Deuteronomy 11:19 | 138 |
| Deuteronomy 15:14 | 5 |
| *Shoftim* | |
| Deuteronomy 16:20 | 56 |
| *Ci Teitzei* | |
| Deuteronomy 22:1-8 | 50 |
| *Ci Tavo* | |
| Deuteronomy 28 | 126 |
| Deuteronomy 28:15 | 72 |

| | |
|---|---|
| *Ha'azinu* | |
| Deuteronomy 32:9-10 | 129 |
| Deuteronomy 32:12 | 174 |
| Deuteronomy 32:46 | 120 |

## Nevi'im

| | |
|---|---|
| 1 Samuel 1:9 | 147 |
| 1 Samuel 16:14 | 147 |
| 2 Samuel 6 | 79 |
| 1 Kings 8 | 86 |
| 1 Kings 17 | 90 |
| 2 Kings 2 | 91 |
| Isaiah 2:2 | 21 |
| Isaiah 11:9 | 21 |
| Isaiah 40 | 172 |
| Isaiah 49:6 | 42 |
| Jeremiah 29:7 | 33,57 |
| Ezekiel 1:5 | 147 |
| Amos 5:24 | 33 |
| Amos 9:7 | 63 |
| Micah 6:6-8 | 10 |
| Zechariah 4:6 | 145 |
| Zechariah 8:16 | 43 |
| Malachi 3:23-24 | 66,91 |
| Malachi 4:24 | 12 |

## Ketuvim

| | |
|---|---|
| Psalm 16:8 | 151 |
| Psalm 41:2 | 61 |
| Psalm 78 | 74 |
| Psalm 105 | 74 |
| Psalm 106 | 74 |
| Psalm 135 | 74 |
| Proverbs 20:27 | 133 |
| Ecclesiastes (Kohelet) 1 | 170 |
| 2 Chronicles 36:21 | 12 |

## Mishnah

| | |
|---|---|
| Avot 2:5-6 | 33 |
| Avot 5:10 | 14 |

| | |
|---|---|
| Bava Metzia 4:12 | 62 |
| Pesachim 10 | 65 |
| Pesachim 10:4 | 67 |
| Pesachim 10:5 | 87 |
| Shabbbat 7:2 | 122 |
| Sotah 3:4 | 139 |
| Sotah 7:1 | 81 |
| Sotah 8:7 | 21 |

## Babylonian Talmud

| | |
|---|---|
| Arachin 17a | 144 |
| Berachot 13a | 81 |
| Berachot 55a | 145 |
| Berachot 61a | 42 |
| Eiruvin 13b | 158 |
| Eiruvin 43b | 92 |
| Gittin 61a | 57 |
| Menachot 43b | 113 |
| Nedarim 39b-40a | 148 |
| Pesachim 99b | 66 |
| Sanhedrin 56a | 158 |
| Sotah 32b | 81 |
| Sotah 35a | 71 |
| Yoma 86a | 31 |

## Midrashic Literature

| | |
|---|---|
| Bemidbar (Numbers) Rabbah 4:20 | 71 |
| Bemidbar (Numbers) Rabbah 11:5 | 6 |
| Bereshit (Genesis) Rabbah 3:7 | 41 |
| Bereshit (Genesis) Rabbah 58:1 | 146 |
| Bereshit (Genesis) Rabbah 58:4 | 102 |
| Bereshit (Genesis) Rabbah 58:5 | 147 |
| Mechilta de Rabbi Ishmael Ex 19:2 | 128 |
| Shemot (Exodus) Rabbah 36:1 | 135 |
| Sifre Deuteronomy 49 | 3 |
| Vayikra (Leviticus) Rabbah 9:9 | 21 |
| Vayikra (Leviticus) Rabbah 24:1 | 61 |

## Mishneh Torah

| | |
|---|---|
| Hil. Keriat Shema 2:10 | 82 |
| Hil. Matanot Aniyim 10:7-14 | 51 |

## Shulchan Aruch

| | |
|---|---|
| Orach Chayyim 62:2 | 82 |
| Orach Chayyim 101:4 | 82 |
| Orach Chayyim 185:1 | 82 |

# GLOSSARY

**Afikomen** – A piece of **Matzah**, the unleavened bread eaten on **Pesach** which is hidden during the **Seder** for a child to find after the meal. May have had a different meaning during the period of the **Mishnah**.

**Amidah** – The central prayer of every Jewish service. It is formed of nineteen blessings on weekdays and seven on **Shabbat**. Sometimes called the **Tefillah** (the prayer) due to its status.

**Bar Mitzvah/Bat Mitzvah** – In **Progressive Judaism** a child becomes Bar or Bat Mitzvah at age thirteen (in **Orthodox Judaism** boys at age thirteen and girls at age twelve). This means that they are now responsible for their own performance of the **mitzvot**. Their coming of age is celebrated by the child being called up to read **Torah** for the first time in their community after a process of learning. Girls are not called up to read **Torah** in **Orthodox Judaism**.

**Baeck, Leo** – (1873-1956). German **Reform** rabbi and religious thinker. Taught at the Hochschule für die Wissenschaft des Judentums in Berlin. Leader of German Jewry before and during the Nazi period, he stayed with his congregation until he was sent to Theresienstadt. He survived and settled in England in 1945. Works include *The Essence of Judaism* and *This People Israel*.

**Bayit Cham** – (Warm house) This term is used in some communities to describe an especially welcoming environment for members of that community, such as a shared meal.

**BCE** – See **Common Era**

**Bimah** – A high place in the **synagogue** from which the service is conducted and the **Torah** read.

**Birkat HaMazon** – The prayers of thanksgiving which end a meal in traditional Jewish practice. Especially used at a **simcha** in order to emphasise the special Jewish character of the meal. Typically sung with great gusto.

**Bubba** – Fond Yiddish name for grandmother.

**CE** – See **Common Era**

**Charoset** – A concoction of fruits, sweet wine and nuts made to look like mortar which is used as a dip during a **Seder**. Recipes vary between different Jewish communities.

**Chassid** – Member of a popular pietistic and mystical movement in Judaism that developed in Eastern Europe in the eighteenth century. Nowadays often distinguishable due to the black and white clothing which is worn exclusively by devotees. Alternatively, and especially in pre-eighteenth-century uses, this term denotes a pious person of no particular affiliation.

181

**Cheder** – (Room) Traditional name for the supplementary school in which Jewish children are educated in the ways of Judaism and the Hebrew language. Classes would often take place in a room off the **synagogue**, hence the name.

**Christian Bible** – Known by Christians as the New Testament, the Christian Bible includes the four Gospels, the Acts and Epistles of the Apostles.

**Chuppah** – The canopy under which a Jewish wedding is conducted, though the word is often used to refer to the whole Jewish wedding ceremony.

**Common Era** – A way of referring to years in the BC/AD system without linking them to the life story of Jesus. Abbreviated BCE for before the Common Era and CE for Common Era.

**Conservative Judaism** – A major denomination of Judaism in the USA and represented in the UK by Masorti Judaism, Masorti being the Hebrew for Conservative. Whilst sharing with **Reform Judaism** an understanding that God's will is revealed progressively, Conservative practice is closer in form to **Orthodox Judaism**.

**Dayan/Dayanim** – A dayan is a Jewish religious judge, especially expert in **Halachah**. **Dayenu** – (Enough for us) A song sung during the **Seder** in which the people gathered together for the meal relate the stages of the Exodus from Egypt, saying that for God to have enabled our ancestors to complete any of them would have been enough.

**D'var Torah** – A personal interpretation of a **Torah** portion written for or said by a Jew to a congregation.

**Glasnost and Perestroika** – The late 1980s policies of openness and reform in the USSR, promulgated by President Mikael Gorbachev, which led to the freedom of Soviet Jews to emigrate and to practice Judaism.

**Haftarah/Haftarot** – Verses from the books of the Prophets which are read on **Shabbat** and festivals after the reading of the Torah. The selection of verses is often suggested by themes from the Torah portion, though at some times of the year they are specific to the season.

**Haggadah** – (Narration) The book which contains the ritual, prayers and story of the **Pesach Seder**. Over the centuries there has been considerable artistic and literary creativity in the creation of its editions.

**Halachah** – The corpus of Jewish law which, for observant Jews, governs all aspects of life.

**Havdalah** – Brief ceremony of separation between the Sabbath and the rest of the week, separating holy and normal time.

**Hebrew Bible** – Known by Christians as the Old Testament, see **Tanach.**

**High Holy Days** – Expression used to denote **Rosh Hashanah** and **Yom Kippur**, the two most widely attended days of the Jewish year.

**Holocaust** – see **Shoah.**

**Kabbalah** – The tradition of Jewish mysticism developed over two millennia. Some of the best-known works of Kabbalah are the Zohar, compiled in Spain in the thirteenth century, and the teachings of the Kabbalists of Safed in the sixteenth century, led by Rabbi Isaac Luria.

**Kaddish** – A prayer mostly in Aramaic which declares God's holiness. It is used in various forms in the Jewish service, to end a section of the service. The word is commonly used to refer to the mourners' Kaddish, when the prayer is recited in memory of those who have died.

**Kashrut** – The Jewish system of eating, literally meaning "fit" or "proper" eating. Kashrut is best known for its prohibitions on eating pig and shellfish and mixing milk and meat at a meal.

**Kavannah** – Doing a **Mitzvah** with concentrated intentionality.

**Ketubah** – The document which records the promises made by the partners in a Jewish wedding.

**Kiddush** – The blessing over wine which marks the beginning of the holy time of **Shabbat**. Sometimes the expression is used to refer to the sequence of blessings over the **Shabbat** candles, children, wine and challah bread that begins **Shabbat**. Also used for the complementary ceremony on **Shabbat** morning.

**Kippah/Kippot** – The characteristic Jewish head covering. There are many designs of kippot. They are worn especially for prayer but may be worn at all times. Men customarily wear a kippah and, in **Progressive Judaism,** women are increasingly also observing the custom.

**Liberal Judaism** – Liberal Judaism in the UK began in 1902 as the Jewish Religious Union, a campaigning movement to reinvigorate Jewish spirituality and involvement. Services were held in the vernacular with modern-minded sermons. The first Liberal **synagogue** was founded in 1911.

**Magen David** – (Star of David) A six-pointed star which has become a universal symbol of Judaism, legendarily once on the shields of King David's army but actually little attested until the Middle Ages and popularised by its adoption by the Zionist movement in the late nineteenth century. It was adopted as the symbol of Judaism on the flag of Israel.

**Mah Nishtanah** – (What is the difference) The four questions adapted from Mishnah Pesachim Chapter 10 which are sung or said at a **Pesach Seder** by the youngest able child present, in order to ask the adults there to explain what is special about the night and meal.

**Maimonides** – Moses ben Maimon (1135-1204) was born in Spain, then settled in Cairo. He was a philosopher, halachist and medical doctor. The foremost Jewish authority of his time.

**Manna** – The legendary staple food provided by God daily, except for **Shabbat**, for the Israelites to collect and eat during the Exodus from Egypt.

183

**Matzah** – Unleavened bread eaten by observant Jews on the festival of **Pesach/Passover**.

**Megillah/Megillot** – The five books from the **Tanach** which are read and studied on the Jewish festivals, including Esther, read on Purim, Ruth, read on Shavuot, Kohelet (Ecclesiastes) read on Sukkot, and the Song of Songs, read on **Pesach**.

**Menorah** – A lamp used for ritual purposes. The word normally refers to the seven-branched candlestick which was in the Temple in Jerusalem.

**Messianic Age** – The notional time in the future when the world will have been perfected.

**Mezuzah** – An encased parchment scroll, written by a scribe, with the words of the **Shema** prayer, which is attached to the right-hand doorpost of an observant Jew's home, and, for some Jews, to all of the rooms of the home which can be slept in.

**Midrash/Midrashim** - (Explanation). Rabbinic interpretation that may be either legal (Midrash Halachah) or homiletical (Midrash Aggadah), sometimes expressed in parables. They have as their starting point quotations from **Torah** or other parts of the **Tanach**.

**Minhag** – Time-honoured Jewish custom of a community or of the Jews of a region or country.

**Mishnah** (Learning) - Legal work consisting of rabbinic decisions and interpretations of the **Torah**, and forming the basis of the **Talmud**. Compiled by Judah HaNasi in the second century CE, it is part of the 'Oral Law' as opposed to the 'Written Law.'

**Mitzvah/Mitzvot** – The duties of a Jew. These range from lighting candles on Shabbat evening to visiting the sick, from giving to charity to attending a funeral.

**Musaf** – (Additional) Service added to **Shabbat** and festival morning services which repeats the **Amidah** but on **Rosh Hashanah** and **Yom Kippur** also contains the most characteristic content for the two days, the blowing of the **shofar** on **Rosh Hashanah** and the commemoration of Yom Kippur in Temple times.

**Ner Tamid** – (Everlasting light) Lamp which burns, or nowadays is often powered by electricity, placed at the front of a **synagogue**. Its origin is the *Ner Tamid* in the Temple in Jerusalem and before that the *Ner Tamid* in the Israelites' portable desert temple.

**Orthodox Judaism** – Orthodox Judaism is made up of number of religious movements. These understand the **Torah** to have been dictated by God to Moses on Mount Sinai and thus only interpretable by a line of authoritative **rabbis** who lead to the **rabbis** of their tradition. They believe that Judaism must keep to the principles and legal decisions of their line of authority.

**Pesach/Passover** – The festival which commemorates the Exodus from Egypt. It takes place in the springtime Hebrew month of Nisan and is observed by **synagogue** services, the **Seder** meal and avoiding the eating of leaven for seven days in Israel and by **Progressive Jews,** or for eight days outside Israel by **Orthodox Jews**.

**Pirke Avot** – (Chapters of the Fathers / Sayings of the Sages) A collection of ethical teachings and aphorisms from the **rabbis** of the time of the **Mishnah**. It is traditionally read on **Shabbat** afternoons.

**Progressive Judaism** – The collective term for **Reform** and **Liberal Judaism**, established by the 1926 foundation of the World Union for Progressive Judaism. Brings together Jewish movements worldwide which understand God's will to be revealed progressively, in order that Jews can respond to their times, rather than as a single event on Mount Sinai.

**Promised Land** – The Land of Israel, to which the Israelite slaves, having escaped from Egypt, were heading. Also figurative of a destination in space or time where a better life can be enjoyed.

**Rabbi/Rabbis** – A rabbi today can be a combination of a scholar, teacher, community leader and community organiser within the Jewish community. Where the word rabbi is capitalised in the text it denotes either the title of a particular contemporary rabbi or the Rabbis of the period of the compilation of the **Mishnah** and **Talmud**.

**Rashi** – (Rabbi Solomon ben Isaac) (1040-1105) French rabbi and leading scholar of his age. His commentary accompanied the first printed edition of the Hebrew Bible. His **Talmud** commentary is still considered the standard tool for its study.

**Reform Judaism** – The first Reform service was held in 1810 in Seesen in Germany. There are now over 1.5 million Reform Jews throughout the world. They understand the **Torah** to have been the work of people aiming to discern the will of God through tamid and *mitzvot*. They believe that Judaism must change and develop to be able to contribute to the world as it is.

**Refusnik** – A Jew in the Union of Soviet Socialist Republics who had applied for a visa to emigrate to Israel and who was refused permission by the Soviet government. *Refusniks* were then often held in limbo for many years, denied employment and other rights and privileges.

**Rosh Hashanah** – The Jewish New Year, a day marked by attending services in the **synagogue** which include the blowing of the **Shofar**.

**Seder** – (Order) The ceremonial meal shared on the first, and, for some Jews, second night of the festival of **Passover (Pesach)**. It is often a time to be together with extended family.

**Sedra** – Also known as Parashah. One of the fifty-four portions into which the **Torah** is divided for reading each year, starting with Bereshit (Genesis Chapters 1:1-6:8) on the first **Shabbat** after the Simchat Torah festival.

**Semichah** – Rabbinic ordination performed by the laying on of hands by a mentor rabbi to a future rabbi after a long process of study and training.

**Shabbat** – The seventh day of the Jewish week, running from sunset on Friday night to the appearance of three stars on Saturday night. The day of rest, the Sabbath. The services that **synagogues** hold on Friday night and Saturday morning are the best attended of the week.

**Shabbat HaGadol** – The **Shabbat** immediately preceding the festival of **Pesach**. It was traditionally a time for a **rabbi** to deliver a sermon on **Pesach** observance.

**Shechitah** – Slaughtering an animal according to the laws of **Kashrut**. The expert who does this is called a Shochet.

**Shema** – Declaration of God's unity, said by an observant Jew morning and evening and thus part of those services. It is formed from three paragraphs in the books of Deuteronomy and Numbers, is the content of the scroll placed in the **Mezuzah**, and is the deathbed declaration.

**Shivah** – The period of seven days after a funeral when Jewish mourning rituals encourage mourners to stay at home together, with family and friends visiting to comfort them. The daily services of the **synagogue** then take place at their home. The word is often taken to denote the evening service taking place at a mourner's home, typically in **Reform** Jewish practice for one to three nights.

**Shlichim** – Emissaries of one Jewish community or movement to another Jewish community or movement.

**Shoah** – The deliberate murder of six million Jews and hundreds of thousands of other people, including Roma and Gay people, by the Nazis in Germany and Eastern Europe during the Second World War. This term is preferred by most Jews to "Holocaust" as it denotes catastrophe rather than any sense of sacrifice.

**Shofar** – A ram's horn which is blown for ritual purposes to sound out a set of traditional musical phrases to mark the beginning of the Jewish New Year on **Rosh Hashanah**.

**Shul** – A fond Yiddish name for **synagogue**.

**Siddur** – The daily and **Shabbat** prayer book.

**Simcha** – A happy occasion, typically a wedding or **Bar** or **Bat Mitzvah**. This word is often used especially to refer to the party afterwards.

**Sukkah** – The temporary shelter built by Jews in observance of the festival of Sukkot. Given Sukkot's harvest celebration, it is typically covered with leaves, fruit and vegetables. Traditionally, meals were eaten there and it was used to sleep in. In **Reform** Jewish practice **synagogues** build Sukkahs for the whole community to use.

**Synagogue** – The Jewish community's combined prayer, learning and community centre. In Britain, the majority of Jews belong to a local **synagogue** of their choice, holding a membership in that **synagogue**. Some are the religious centre for just a few people and some for thousands.

**Tallit** – The prayer shawl worn by observant Jews for morning services and on a few other occasions. Characteristically striped with four **Tzitzit** hanging down from each corner, with eight threads and five knots representing the five books of the **Torah**.

**Talmud** – (Teaching) Compilation of the commentaries of the Rabbis on the **Mishnah** from the second to fifth centuries CE, covering both religious and civil matters. A mixture of laws, customs, discussions, stories and sayings, it became the foundation of Jewish practice throughout the world. There are two versions, the Yerushalmi (Jerusalem), compiled in Palestine and completed in about four hundred CE, and the Bavli, compiled in Babylon and completed between five hundred and eight hundred CE. The Bavli is regarded as being authoritative.

**Tanach** – the Hebrew Bible composed of the **Torah** (Genesis to Deuteronomy), the Nevi'im (the Prophets, from the book of Samuel to Malachi, the last of the Prophets) and Ketuvim (the writings from Psalms to the Second Book of Chronicles and including the **Megillot** for the Jewish festivals).

**Tefillah** – (Prayer) The word can mean any prayer, the whole process of prayer, or specifically the prayers of the **Amidah.**

**Torah** – The five books of Moses, Genesis, Exodus, Leviticus, Numbers and Deuteronomy, which are the foundational text of Judaism, read every **Shabbat** in **synagogue.**

**Tsourises** – Yiddish words for troubles that a person encounters in life.

**Tzedakah** – The Jewish duty to ensure balance between the rich and the poor by giving to the needy.

**Tzitzit** – Knotted strings which hang from the four corners of a **Tallit.** There are eight strings in each corner held together in five knots to represents the books of the **Torah.**

**Ulpan** – A learning institute for the intensive study of modern Hebrew. Most are in Israel and are aimed at teaching the language to new immigrants.

**World To Come** – Part of the Jewish eschatology. This world is considered to be in need of deep repair, the World To Come is a world of perfection.

**Yahrzeit** – The Jewish tradition of marking the anniversary of the death of a close relative. It is observed by lighting a candle and saying a memorial prayer.

**Yeshiva** – Traditional Jewish study institute in which classical Jewish texts are studied, in **Orthodox Judaism** only for men and primarily aimed at young adults.

**Yom HaAtzmaut** – Day which celebrates annually the declaration of independence of the State of Israel in 1948.

**Yom HaShoah** – Day which commemorates annually the **Shoah.** The day was fixed by the Israeli Knesset (Parliament) to coincide with the day that the Warsaw Ghetto uprising began.

**Yom HaZikaron** – Day which commemorates annually those who have died in defence of the State of Israel. Always the day before **Yom HaAtzmaut.**

**Yom Kippur** – The Day of Atonement, on which Jews repent for their sins of the past year. Normally the largest gathering of the **synagogue** year. Observant Jews fast on this day.

*Some entries are adapted from those in the glossaries of the Siddurim and Machzorim of the Movement for Reform Judaism.*

# BIBLIOGRAPHY

Baeck, Leo, *The Essence of Judaism* (New York: Shocken Books, 1948)

Borowitz, Eugene, *A Touch of the Sacred* (Woodstock: Jewish Lights, 2009)

Borts, Barbara & Tikvah Sarah, Elli, *Women Rabbis in the Pulpit* (London: Kulmus, 2015)

Fishkoff, Sue, *The Rebbe's Army* (New York: Shocken Books, 2005)

Greenspoon, Leonard, ed., *Rites of Passage* (West Lafayette: Purdue University Press, 2010)

Gryn, Hugo, *Chasing Shadows* (London: Viking, 2000)

Heschel, Abraham Joshua, *The Sabbath* (New York: Farrar, Straus and Giroux, 1951)

Hoffman, Lawrence & Bradshaw, Paul, eds, *Life Cycles in Jewish and Christian Worship* (University of Notre Dame Press, 1996)

Montefiore, Claude, *The Bible for Home Reading, Part 1* (London: Forgotten Books, 2016)

Rayner, John, *Jewish Religious Law: A Progressive Perspective* (London: Berghahn Books, 1998)

Sacks, Jonathan, The Home We Build Together (London: Continuum, 2007)

Salkin, Jeffrey, Being God's Partner (Woodstock: Jewish Lights, 1994)

Schachter-Shalomi, Zalman, First Steps to a New Jewish Spirit (Woodstock: Jewish Lights, 2003)

Telushkin, Joseph, ed., Jewish Wisdom (New York: William Morrow, 1994)

Zion, Noam & Dishon, David, A Different Night – A Family Participation Haggadah (Jerusalem: Shalom Hartman, 1997)

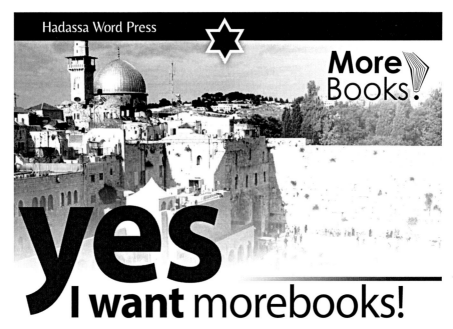 

Printed by
**Schaltungsdienst Lange o.H.G., Berlin**